Still Life at Eighty

Still Life at Eighty

A MEMOIR

NICHOLAS DELBANCO

[M]

MANDEL VILAR PRESS

This book is typeset in Masqualero 12/17. The paper used in this book meets the minimum requirements of ANSI/NISO Z39.48-1992 (R1997). ♾

Text and cover designed by Sophie Appel

Unless otherwise noted, photos are from the personal collection of Nicholas Delbanco.

Publisher's Cataloging-in-Publication Data
Names: Delbanco, Nicholas, 1942–, author.
Title: Still life at eighty: a memoir
Description: Simsbury, Connecticut: Mandel Vilar Press, 2024. |
Includes 32 black & white photographs
Identifiers: ISBN 9781942134985 (softcover with French flaps) |
ISBN 9781942134992 (eBook)
Subjects: Nicholas Delbanco, memoir / Literary figures, 20th and 21st century / Art and artifacts / Family and houses.
Classification: LCC PS3554.E442 S240 2024

Printed in the United States of America
24 25 26 27 28 29 30 31 32 33 34 / 9 8 7 6 5 4 3 2 1

Mandel Vilar Press
19 Oxford Court, Simsbury, Connecticut 06070
www.mvpublishers.org | www.americasforconservation.org

For Elena

On August 27, 2022, I became eighty years old. According to the calendar, I've been alive not merely for years but decades, centuries, and even millennia: 1942 seems very long ago. In the way of such things, however, it also feels like yesterday; time both flies and crawls. So I want to use the occasion of my birthday to consider days and years behind, as well as those to come.

A recent piece by Paul Theroux, "On Turning Eighty" (2021) and one by V. S. Pritchett, "The Turning of the Years" (1982), stand as models for me, though there are many others. To take only a small sampling, we have work by Roger Angell, Simone de Beauvoir, Ursula K. Le Guin, Donald Hall, and Grace Paley on the topic of old age. It's a function of the writer's life that there be interaction between the public and the private spheres; one hopes the latter may reflect upon or refract the former. This is a personal essay (as in the root meaning of Old French essai), but written for the eyes of others: an *attempt*. It's both a summing-up and forward-facing effort: May it suggest finality but not be the last word.

PART I

Time and Place

I have owned seven houses. I've lived in at least seven more. This does not count apartments rented, dormitories occupied, hotels and motels. My life has not been more than most a wanderer's, but at this stage I cannot tally all the roofs I've lain beneath; they number in the hundreds, surely, and plausibly the thousands. On a trip around the world in my late twenties, I slept in dozens of beds. Some of them were memorable and stay vivid; more of them have blurred and gone indistinct.

This is a function of increasing age and scarcely a surprise. But one of the habits of old age—also unsurprising—is the way we look back not forward; it's retrospect not prospect that's the governing perspective of the period. We mark our time in several ways and by several markers: our salary, our sex life, our friendships and health and political engagement and family and geography and homes. This last will be my focus here.

The triad "food, clothing, and shelter" is a commonplace of speech and a common set of requirements. The third of these, whether new or patched together or rebuilt, is nonetheless our cover in rain and heavy weather. If the roof is tile or stone or slate or wood shingle or asphalt or thatch or concrete or interwoven branches or tin, we may infer something about the location and the wherewithal of those who lie beneath. A lean-to and a palace share an overarching element: each is a protective structure stretching "up above my head."

What stretched above my head were all sorts of roofs, though that's more a function of time than change; I'd guess most people at this stage of life can make an equivalent claim. The rich own several houses concurrently; the poor may never own one. Some people are habitual travelers; others stay at home. But in our age of mass migration and ready transport, most are nomadic again. It's the rare elder who has, all her or his existence, remained beneath a constant ceiling and in a single shelter. When we say, "The roof fell in," we describe catastrophe; when we say, "Raise high the roof beam," we're voicing a fond hope.

If Shakespeare's claim stays true that there are seven ages in the full span of a player's life, then one house owned per decade may well be representative. Those who move much more often are more often tenants than owners. My pride of ownership varied; some houses I delighted in or failed to, but each is a receptacle of memory.

So I want to list them here. These were not family houses—the ones my parents came from or homes to which they moved. Glancingly, I write of space occupied in childhood, but only to report on furniture and paintings, not the structures that contained them. Nor do I refer to houses I lived in that belonged to other people—in the south of England, for example, or the coast of California, or (except in passing, when I describe a lunch party) the south of France. Rather, the roofs I focus on were ones I chose myself when I attained "a man's estate," and the sight line is rear-facing and chronological.

All of the buildings still stand.

The first such structure was a farm I bought in 1969, at the tender age of twenty-six, in Washington County, New York. In our time of pinpoint accuracy and Google maps, I can be more specific: It sat at the crest of Spraguetown Road, in the village of Greenwich—pronounced with a long "e," unlike the decidedly more upscale town in Connecticut—and the intersecting street at the property's edge went by the name of North Road. The latter is an uphill track that led, after a steep downhill, to Cossayuna, a hamlet a mile distant. "Rock Hill" comprised all the land I could see: roughly a hundred acres, since the house dated from the early 1820s, when the land had been measured not in acreage but "chains," a surveyor's term then current. It had been built at the base of the hill, so the surrounding view was of a dell.

Washington County remains one of the poorest rural areas of upstate New York, though upscale Saratoga Springs lies no great distance away. My neighbors were farmers or mechanics in trailers, but the house itself was, in its modest way, grand: brick, slate-roofed, with four chimneys and large windows built in the style of Queen Anne. It had been owned, to start with, by a founding family of the village, when Greenwich was called "Tuckerstown." There were marble markers of the graves of Tuckers on a knoll above the pond. In addition to the house itself, there was a large hay barn and several outbuildings: a garage, a milking shed, a toolshed, and an outhouse from the days before indoor plumbing, also roofed in slate. The nearby quarries, in Granville, New York, and Danby, Vermont, meant this now-expensive roofing material came cheap at the time of construction; the barn's roof was patterned slate. And though more than a half century has passed, and inflation happens everywhere (what happened to the five-cent cigar, or the three-thousand-dollar car? The codger in me grumbles), the place was a pure bargain. I paid a little less than thirty thousand dollars for the property known as Rock Hill Farm: tools and stacks of firewood and outbuildings and pond and meadows and woodlots and stone walls and silo and graveyard and all.

I was born in England, not America. My parents were not native to England but to Germany. The family name is Italian. So transience was the rule not the exception of my early history, and at a certain point in young adulthood I felt the need for roots not lateral but vertical.

It was a time when many urbanites dreamed they might go "back to nature," and the house in Greenwich (a thirty-mile drive from Bennington College, where I taught) was, for me, affordable. I settled in and settled down and pretended—avidly, incompetently—to be a farmer. I did learn the difference between a sheep and a goat, a turnip and a rutabaga; I tried to shore up the fallen field-bordering walls, then leased the land to a near neighbor who wanted extra pasture for his herd of Holsteins. I had a chunk stove in the kitchen and fed it cords of wood I split, but it was all play-acting and I was never good at it. The whole was an adventure.

Soon enough I got engaged and married and, after a few years, Elena and I had a child. Francesca was born in a nearby hospital, the only infant in Mary McLellan's maternity ward. We painted her bedroom bright yellow and built bookshelves for her books and toys; we "child-proofed" the sockets and stairs. We recited "Old MacDonald Had a Farm," and read the Peter Rabbit books but avoided the story of Bambi, which seemed to us too sad. In high heels on the rutted roads, my wife pushed an Italian pram while our daughter slept within. In miniskirts she planted and hoed the furrows of peas and potatoes. The hospital closed down.

What remains for me, in memory, is Rock Hill's interior, the work we did on demolition and, with the expert help of builders, renovation. The house had been a warren of small and ill-proportioned rooms; we left only bearing walls. We trebled the size of the kitchen and added a porch overlooking the stream. The living room—once three separate enclosures, with an entry hall and stairwell—became a single, open space, a spiral stairwell in the center. Getting that black spiral stair with its protective railing through the entry door was no easy matter; it had been built in Arlington, Vermont, by a man whose business was just such construction, and who assured me it could be carried through a standard aperture. He was right, but only barely; we had to corkscrew the heavy metal object through the front door of the house, then lever it upright and into basement footings. This took four men, and it took all my self-control not to recite, as we hauled and heaved and positioned it, "The Winding Stair" by William Butler Yeats.

In short order we had what seemed to me the only loft within two hundred miles of Houston Street, its windows giving out on meadows and pine trees and, at some distance, the road. There was a Rumford fireplace in a west-facing chimney and two acorn stoves upstairs. We dredged the pond and stocked it with Muscovy ducks. I built myself a third-floor studio, recalling Thoreau's injunction to "go up attic," and it's not an accident I've cited two of my literary heroes in these last two paragraphs: This was the house my first book bought, and where I continued to write. Indeed, my fifth novel, *In the Middle Distance* (1971), tracks closely though in fictive terms the destruction and the reconstruction process. I wrote the book at twenty-nine, imagining a forty-eight-year-old called Nicholas Delbanco who inhabited Rock Hill. He had my name and passport number and, to some degree, my past; his future was invented, but the details of remodeling were real. The whole procedure—steaming off layers of wallpaper, pulling up linoleum and sanding the wide pine planks beneath—seemed to me a metaphor for the structure of the self. And though this sounds pretentious I did feel I took ownership of who I was and wanted to become by exposing the beams and plastering the ceilings and planing the doors and painting the walls of the previous residents' home.

It was a beautiful place. We were very happy there. Yet, as an effete friend observed, it was "terrifyingly authentic," by which he meant that thirty miles was not only a difficult winter's drive to the college where we worked, but also a world away. The "natives" were not neighborly but suspicious of city-slicker behavior; we were the only Jews and Democrats within long hailing distance. The Greenwich police would wait at a curve on Spraguetown Road to ticket our visitors, with their out-of-state plates and fancy cars, for speeding. By the time our daughter Francesca was ready for school, it wasn't a school to which we wished to send her, and the cracks in the plaster and leaks in the gutter and worn-down marble lintels lost their charm. The rooms were hard to heat; bats swooped down from the chimneys and flitted past my sleeping wife; wasps nested in the eaves. A fox killed all our ice-bound ducks; the stone walls continued collapsing, and the magisterial elm by the barn succumbed to Dutch elm disease. So we rented out, then sold the house and moved instead to what became our second home, a renovated barn in North Bennington, Vermont.

It sat at the edge of the campus of Bennington College, where I taught from 1966 to 1985. The barn itself had been rebuilt and moved to a site above a meadow that gave out on a distant view of the Green Mountains and the Glastonbury Pass. Constructed for a past president of the college, and known as "Leigh House" in his honor, it too had no visible neighbors, though the surrounding roads were more heavily trafficked than had been the case for Rock Hill.

The ground floor was a single large room, nearly fifty feet by thirty feet, with a two-story central apse and haymows up above that had been transformed into bedrooms and bathrooms; it still had the feel of a farm structure, with rafters and beaming exposed. When the building had served as the president's house, it doubled as reception space, its kitchen tucked into a corner underneath the stairs. Since Mrs. Leigh had had no desire to cook, the dining service sent over their meals. Elena, however, soon became expert at large-scale entertainments, cooking routinely for a dozen and often for seventy-five.

At first we paid rent to the college; then, when I became director of a summer program, the Bennington Summer Writing Workshops, we lived in Leigh House rent-free. We did much entertaining there, and tried to raise funds for the program and school, since the house was a showplace of sorts.

Once, I remember, the president of Bennington brought over a Hollywood mogul who'd made a killing with a TV series and was ready to be someone's patron, if they paid adequate suit.

We plied the man with drinks. The long view out over the mountains was both austere and picturesque; a full moon began its ascent.

As it did so, the house lights went out. They did this often, at the slightest puff of wind, because the electricity was—to be generous—erratic. We locals stood in the dark unconcerned and watched the rising moon. That orb, resplendent, rose. After ten minutes or so, once the harvest moon had cleared the cleft of Glastonbury Pass and filled the night sky, gleaming, the lights of the room went back on. The mogul turned to me and said, meaning it, "You people really understand the way to stage things. What an effect!"

Again, I fashioned a studio under the eaves and wrote there happily, staring out across the meadow and the maple trees. Our second daughter, Andrea, was born. We acquired a dog and a cat. When the college went into one of its periodic spasms of near-bankruptcy and de-accessioning of buildings and land, we bought the house. Expanding it—enlarging the kitchen and adding a screened porch—we made the property our own. Adding a chunk stove to the fireplace chimney (the aptly named "Defiant" from Vermont Castings), we again burned cords of wood and huddled in cold evenings on a nearby couch. Late night poker games and holiday revels—carved pumpkins and high-raked leaf piles and, when the snows came, cross-country ski treks out the kitchen door—all stay etched in recollection as the generous spirit of place. Leigh House had, in abundance, what some describe as fêng shui. The slope of the meadow was gradual, graceful; a stand of pines behind the building protected it from drive-by sighting from College Road. Two birch trees supported a hammock; large bushes of hydrangea flanked the entrance drive.

Once again, I loved the interior space, its intimate grandeur, its blend of the folksy and formal, its graphic art and photographs and masks on every wall. Of the seven houses I here list, this one felt most like home to me—the place where our daughters declared themselves as personalities (and where Andrea would get married), the place where I wrote *Sherbrookes,* my trilogy of novels about a clan of Vermonters, the place where Elena and I could cultivate our garden and grow practiced at the marriage-dance as we entered middle-age. The Bennington Summer Writing Workshops and the low-residency MFA in Creative Writing—for both of which I served as founding director—brought a host of friends and semi-strangers to our table. It was a halcyon time.

These lines deal with houses not people, but it is of course the people who create and imbue the spirit of place. Just to list a smattering of "Johns" who sat at that table is to spell old ghosts:

John Ashbery, John Cheever, John Gardner, John Irving, John Frederick Nims, John Updike were among our glad companions there, and of that half dozen only one, John Irving, remains alive. Of the "Marys"—Mary Robison, Mary Ruefle, and Mary Lee Settle, to name three who graced our gatherings (not to mention Grace Paley), the first two quick, the last two dead—all of them remain, in memory, under the one roof.

Once, I remember, Donald Barthelme was visiting the workshop, and came to the kitchen door at seven o'clock in the morning. "Do you have any bouillon?" he asked me, bleary-eyed. He carried a bottle of vodka, most of which he'd drunk the night before, and needed what he called a bull shot to steady his outstretched hand.

"What's a 'bull shot?'" I inquired.

He looked at me with amused condescension. "Vodka, beef broth. The hair of the dog."

I did have a can of consommé and rummaged for it through the shelves. Then John Gardner stumbled down from the attic, where he'd been sleeping in my studio, and soon enough the two of them were shouting at each other. In his just-released *On Moral Fiction* (1978), Gardner had savaged Barthelme's writing as an example of the frivolity in art that he despised. Barthelme did not take kindly to having been insulted in print, and the pair were close to blows when a third writer, Frederick Busch, came in.

Busch, stone-cold sober, was a member of our Writing Workshop faculty, and a creature of habit who wanted strong coffee to begin his day; he'd stopped by, he told me, to borrow a grinder and pot. These three large men—two of them big-bellied, one tall—stood in the kitchen arguing, when my wife arrived in her diaphanous nightgown to say the kids were sleeping and the shouting was too loud.

This quieted them. Barthelme departed, with his can of consommé. Gardner withdrew again to bed, and Busch went to his studio with the makings of espresso. All three of them are dead. Elena said, "Enough's enough," and retired to check on the children, silk billowing behind her. From then on out we had a rule: No writers in the house till ten . . .

For years and even decades, after we'd moved to Michigan, we shared ownership of Leigh House with another couple, who lived there as retirees while we were working elsewhere, then spent summers and holiday seasons with their own children when we returned. The only drawback of this arrangement was how much we liked our fellow-owners, and over time, as they aged and grew less mobile, we cohabited as couples in the single structure. They built an additional ground-floor bedroom and wheelchair-accessible bathroom once they could no longer climb the stairs.

When, three years ago, our surviving elder partner died and the place went on the market, it was as if we bade farewell to an entire epoch and album of fond memories: all those dinner parties and loud drunken revels, all those winter nights when the Defiant needed stoking, all those arguments and passionate agreements when the world was young.

"We have heard the chimes at midnight, Master Shallow," as Shakespeare's Falstaff says. Elsewhere, in the voice of Prospero, the Bard declares, "Our revels now are ended." Both these lines are composed for and spoken by older actors, and both embody attitudes of at-least-middle age. The house we bought in Ann Arbor, Michigan, when we moved there with our children, dog, and cat in 1985, was very much the house of an established, tax-paying family, not a house in the middle of nowhere or a remodeled barn. It too was brick, though the brick had been white-washed, and there were only two chimneys. It too gave out on a rarely-traveled road, dead-ending in Ann Arbor's famed Arboretum, so I was able to persuade myself that we still lived in the country and could take long walks with Major Scobie, my beloved dog.

428 Concord Road was, it turned out when I checked the town's tax records, the only house on Concord Road itself. Though this time we had neighbors, we could see out every window. All those adjacent houses had their front doors facing other streets in our little cul-de-sac, and their postal location used the other names. So I asked the town authorities if our mailing address could just be "Concord Road."

"No," the clerk said. "You're 428."

"But there's no 426 or 430," I protested.

"Sir, your house is 428."

"Why can't I be #1 Concord Road? Or 100 Concord Road? Or an interesting number like, say, 666?"

"You're on a grid."

"What's that?"

The clerk was losing patience. "According to the city map, you're in the quadrant of 400 numbers. And the fire department needs to be able to find you, and the water and the sewer people and the electric company. You're 428."

We settled down and settled in and made of the structure a home. Where first we possessed a hundred acres and later, in Vermont, fifteen, the lot on Concord Road was barely a third of an acre. Nonetheless, and in the strange economy of *location, location, location*, it was far and away the most expensive of the properties we'd owned. The building could have been designed as a mail order catalogue copy of a faux-colonial house, and it was vaguely reminiscent of the one on Spraguetown Road.

This time I knew enough to leave well enough alone and bring down no walls. A central hall and stairwell faced the entrance door; a wood-paneled study that might once have served as a parlor sat at the corridor's end. There was a living room on the south side, a dining room and kitchen to the north. There was a basement "family room" and, on the second floor, three bedrooms and two small bathrooms, as well as a fourth bedroom which I encircled with bookshelves and made my writing space.

It was, said Elena, the house of the three little pigs, not easy to blow down. It withstood wind and weather—a tornado warning sounded our first week in Ann Arbor and, though some trees were leveled in the nearby Arboretum, the house itself stood firm. Once we'd filled it with our art and books and furniture, it fit like a snug glove. The building was constructed in 1938, when materials were solid and the plumblines true. The place felt "safe as houses": a dry basement with a laundry chute, a furnace that worked properly, an air conditioner too. The attached garage was heated, and it held two cars.

Over time we did enlarge the space, refurbishing the basement and adding a wing to the kitchen, then adding a sunroom and studio, where Elena could paint, sew, and write. Some fifteen years in, and after a particularly heavy winter, the roof began to leak. We arranged to have it reshingled, and our laconic Finnish roofer said there were three options; we would have to choose. He offered us a range of thicknesses and costs; he used asphalt shingles guaranteed to last for twenty, or for thirty, or for forty years.

I opted for the second choice: thirty-year shingles. He looked at me disapprovingly: "What? You're not an optimist?"

I said thirty years would do.

Our girls grew up and left for college and then their separate lives. We remained. We loved our cross-fence neighbors and, when they too left, loathed the new arrivals who doubled the size of their structure and blocked out the west-facing light. The dog died, then the cat. The comfort-rounds of habit began to seem like repetition, and Ann Arbor—to a degree—lost its charm. In part because of this, we repeated our experiment in shared ownership, spending less time on Concord Road and buying a house across the state on the shores of great Lake Michigan. This is the fourth house to report on, and a new start of sorts.

"Of sorts" because, by collective agreement, it was a house we occupied and did not own alone. There are various forms of proprietorship—individual, collective, cooperative—and in this case there were four names on the deed from the start. We embarked upon the purchase of the house in Lakeside with a pair of friends from Ann Arbor who had been biking through the region and who, like us, wanted a place to escape to within easy driving distance.

He was the dean of the Taubman College of Architecture and Urban Planning at the University of Michigan, she a painter, and their aesthetic was a modernist one: everything functional, everything spare. Aside from the advantage of shared expense, it seemed to us that co-ownership of a "country home"—a place not inhabited all year round—would give it more use and be less wasteful. One has only to think of how many houses—ski chalets in Utah, condominiums in Florida—stand empty for much of the year (while being heated or air-conditioned) to recognize the inequity of our social and economic system. Hundreds of thousands in America are homeless, living on the street; millions of second homes stand empty when their owners are away. And though shared ownership did not alleviate that problem, it made us feel slightly less guilty while we reveled by the shore...

In the working papers of our LLC (Limited Liability Corporation) we agreed that no household item could be purchased or wall color chosen or bush planted unless the choice was unanimous, and that each addition must be voted on. In one shopping trip to Chicago, the four of us bought all the furniture required for the empty rooms; the local flea markets and galleries offered up the rest. As with Leigh House in Bennington, this private time-share system worked well because we liked and trusted our co-owners, and the times when we "fourgathered" there were always celebratory. 9173 Pier Street in the village of Lakeside began to feel like a new old home.

To call Lakeside a village is to overstate the case. There was nearly nothing there. The large identifying number—9173—

belied the actual length of Pier Street and, like the 428 on Concord Road, had been established for the purpose of mapping vacancy. The lot was almost two acres, and fronted on the street. Lakeside had a post office (although soon enough, in the money-saving consolidation of the United States Postal Service, it would lose that facility), a couple of tony home design shops, a railroad crossing, a single stop sign, and a church.

Our house was known as "the Wilkinson place." An historical marker, planted in the front-facing garden, proclaimed it a Centennial Farm House, inhabited by the same family for one hundred years. It was, in fact, the oldest surviving structure in the village, which itself was once called Wilkinson—reminiscent of the Tucker homestead in what had been Tuckerstown. In the one-room museum of Lakeside, there's a photograph of old man Wilkinson and his wife, standing sternly on their porch and doing a good imitation of Grant Wood's *American Gothic.* They were farmers; they owned apple orchards and, to tend them, slaves. When, after the Civil War, Wilkinson's side lost the battle and he decamped for southern states, the citizens of his eponymous town no longer wished to honor him, and changed the name to "Lakeside." The shoreline of Lake Michigan became, over time, a tourism-based rather than an agricultural economy. Second houses sprouted for Chicago gentry looking to escape the heat in summer; the beachfront "cottages" grew large, and a hotel or two, a golf club, and roadhouse restaurants gave the surrounding area the feel of a resort.

Our property sat eight hundred feet from the shore. The people from whom we purchased it were hoarders, and by the time they listed the place for sale it was impossible to see the "bones" of the building; the downstairs windows were hidden by stacked boxes and layers of floral-patterned curtains, along with used and unused racks of clothes, the porches chocka-block and piled every which way for storage. They had had seven children, though how nine people cohabited there was beyond us to imagine; there were only narrow walkways between the piles of furniture and kitchen plates and lamps.

Because of the high-mounded newspapers and magazines and empty bottles and dead plants, they had been unable to sell. Elena, however, saw past the bric-a-brac's confusion and imagined the place stripped bare; we bought it with the written condition that the house and lawn and outbuildings would have no remnant clutter within. Our contingent offer was a welcome one; the family wanted to move and needed to settle up debts. Dumpster after dumpster and truck after truck emptied out the rooms and free-standing garage; downed trees were carved up and carried away. Antique dealers and flea market proprietors and junk traders turn by turn reduced the stock, and decades of accumulation gave way to subtraction instead.

Our "walk-through" prior to purchase was a revelation: Here were windows we'd not seen before, here a built-in cabinet, here a claw-foot bathtub. For the whole of that first winter, a local carpenter and painter labored over restoration, stripping the detritus of the previous owners' occupancy and painting the walls white. When we took up residence in the late spring of 2004, it was an empty space.

There Elena and I first tasted the pleasures and the drawbacks of Midwestern village life. Since the property bordered Pier Street, a walkway to the public beach, there were neighbors waving as they jogged by and dogs raising legs on the shrubbery and strangers with transistor radios and striped towels strolling past. Our east-facing border gave out on the house and gardens of the Chicago-based architects Stanley Tigerman and Margaret McCurry, and they became real friends.

The west-facing boundary, however, gave onto the home of a retired electrician whose pleasure in the use of power tools and blaring right-wing broadcasts was only equaled by the pleasure he took in tormenting us with them. On one side, therefore, was beauty and peace; on the other a near-open war.

This dynamic may well may be an under-examined aspect of community. At least in the rural or suburban context, who lives next to you is almost as important as the house you occupy. It's the premise of the recent big-screen comedies *Neighbors* and *Neighbors 2*, where a young married couple is bedeviled by a fraternity house and, in the sequel, a sorority house next door. There were many interesting people in the environs of Lakeside, but our combative neighbor—cutting his lawn compulsively on a riding mower and then blowing off the blades of grass with a power blower, power washing his paved driveway, chain sawing branches, and painting and repainting his fence, all the while listening to Rush Limbaugh or religious homilies—put at risk, for us, the "spirit of place."

Over time, the situation grew malign. When we complained to the police about the decibel levels of his machinery, they pointed to the village ordinance that made noise a "public nuisance" only after ten at night; when we played Schubert or Mendelssohn on the porch, he countered by turning his own volume up. At 9:59 on summer evenings he would cut his engines and turn the radio off. I'm aware of how petty and silly this sounds, but our pleasure in the house was calibrated to and dependent on the presence or the absence of the man a lawn away...

Our fifth home, on the outer shores of Cape Cod, was inherited. Elena's parents built it in the early 1950s, and even at that age it's the youngest of this so-far catalogue, a "mid-century modern" edifice at the crest of a steep Wellfleet hill. When they died, the house on Summit Avenue—overlooking a marsh and the harbor—came into our possession. The house had four acres of land, with commanding views and total privacy and ample proportions and interior space; we could never have afforded to buy it on our own.

This was, again, a large step up in terms of valuation from where we'd lived before. It was a generous legacy, but a complicated one. For openers, it seemed excessive and beyond our means to own property both by the Atlantic Ocean and on a Great Lake. So we sold the house in Lakeside—ruefully, though with an admixture of relief—and moved, again, back east.

In fact we'd owned another house in Wellfleet, years before. As a wedding present, in 1970, Elena's parents deeded us a cottage on a curve of Gull Pond Road, not two miles from their home. The place had charm abounding, and we reveled there. Yet it was a rickety structure, once a woodcutter's heatless shack in the clearing of a stretch of scrub oak, poison ivy, and pitch pine.

Painted dark brown, with red shutters, it had faulty wiring, a less-than-reliable pump, and a leak-prone moss-covered roof.

The stove was a camp stove, the icebox just a slight improvement upon an old-fashioned literal ice box kept chill by sawdust and ice. Although fine and romantic for newlyweds, the cottage was not, as we became parents, somewhere it made sense to stay. Squirrels nested there in winter, and mice foraged all year long; after some summers of tenancy we left the worm-holed structure and stayed in the "big house" instead.

Her parents died in their nineties, and in their final years the home on Summit Avenue suffered from neglect. It had been constructed as a summer place, on a shoestring budget, and was added to when Elena's father—a famed cellist and founding member of The Beaux Arts Trio—grew well heeled. But, as we came to understand when assessing the building for renovation, corners had been cut and poor construction choices made. There was only Homosote soundproofing, for example, no true insulation in the walls; this explained the size of our heating bills in winter. The exterior walls were slathered with protective creosote, no longer a permitted substance, and therefore all the cedar shingles had to be replaced. The porch was a danger to tread on, full of splinters and rotten lumber and ankle-turning holes. Trees threatened the roof in moderate wind and brushed at the windows in gales. An open well in the basement had been covered over with plywood; black mold and mushrooms flourished there, and the garage was dank.

It would have been simple to raze the structure and build something new on the site. But "Casa Verdi" had been Elena's childhood summer home, and though not all the memories were happy ones it seemed to her disloyal to take a wrecking ball to the place where her mother and father had lived. We considered selling the property outright and, after some deliberation, rejected that choice also. It wasn't an easy decision and took time to make.

Although not technically hoarders (as had been the actual case with the owners of the Wilkinson house in Lakeside), her parents had accumulated decades worth of clutter. There were paid bills and cancelled checks and letters and contracts and property deeds and playbills and concert programs and insurance policies stored higgledy-piggledy in cardboard cartons. Broken toasters and portable radios and cracked coffeepots awaited repair; pillows and sets of mismatched plates and glasses abounded in the attic; vinyl records and family photographs and surveyors' maps and unworn shoes and hats and maps and mops and magazines filled each storage closet. For four hours every morning, Elena sifted through the boxes and file folders that held her present past. Each day, in a car stuffed with rejects, I made my way to the thrift shop and dump. It took us two long summers to come to terms with the inheritance and make the decision to resurrect and not sell the house.

We hired a local builder—a white-haired, blue-eyed, whippet-thin New Englander—who had impeccable taste. Tact was not his strong suit, however, and as the owner and proprietor of Wellfleet Custom Builders, Bob Bacon suggested the place should be a teardown. Like most of the builders and craftsmen I've known, he scorned what had been done by predecessors—finding fault with the way the doors were hung and windows glazed, the construction techniques and materials used by those who built before. Hard of hearing—perhaps from years of using power tools—he liked to call me "Professor," and the term was not one of respect. Nevertheless, and after weeks of questioning it, he accepted our desire to rebuild.

That choice entailed a lengthy procedure, and a demanding one. It took the best part of a year. Bob put in insulation and reshingled the exterior walls and ventilated the eaves. He built an outdoor shower and rebuilt the rotting porch. A new electrical entrance with new wiring—the house had had no three-pronged outlets—was installed. The well in the basement was sealed, the septic system flushed. We added windows and solid, as opposed to hollow, wooden doors and painted over the knotty-pine planking and turned the kitchen sink around so it gave out not on a plasterboard partition but on the commanding view. We replaced the warped pine cabinets and shelving and the corroded pipes; we bought a new stove and refrigerator and dehumidifier and upgraded the furnace and the air conditioner and took away cracked linoleum and took down the moth-eaten drapes.

Each month the bills arrived from Wellfleet Custom Builders. Each month there were new faults to find and new decisions to take: what to do with the sagging living room ceiling, what kind of fan or chandelier to hang. By the expensive end of the process, we had retained the footprint of the place but made the house our own; now it's everything we wanted or could want. Each wall has been repainted and every window washed. Where I sit to type these pages has a cherished east- and south-facing exposure out over the gardens and bay. In summertime, with our children and their husbands and our children's children here—now numbering eleven at table—it feels like a permanent home.

It's still Elena's parents' place, however, to the mailman and the plumber and the folks who come to fill the oil tank or service the generator. It will stay that way, I imagine, in the memory of the locals till we in turn give way to those who will succeed us; the man who takes down deadwood or prunes the maple trees or delivers a sack full of oysters is sure to recollect my in-laws and pause to reminisce. No matter how long we lie beneath this roof, it will not shelter us alone but also the couple who built it and now are tenants of the nearby cemetery. The house outlasts us all.

This is, I think, a telling aspect of the history of houses—how they change to fit their occupants, how they "accommodate" the tastes and desires of those with their names on the deed. Each of the homes I describe has been remodeled over time—sometimes a little, sometimes a lot—by those who live there now. It's the rare structure that remains untouched, and even the process of restoration is necessarily one of change, with more or less concern for historic preservation. In a restored nineteenth-century house, for instance, should there be electrical sockets and switches for lights on the walls? Should the light source not be whale oil, or beeswax, or something that antedates Edison? Should the roof have solar panels and the bulbs be LED?

The man who bought our house on Spraguetown Road was a stickler for authenticity, and soon enough he removed the spiral stairwell and the plateglass windows, the acorn stoves and redwood porch; he located the original wallpaper pattern and covered the white walls again and put back the partitions for the several downstairs rooms. Not such an absolutist as to pull out indoor plumbing and the electrical entrance, he nonetheless filled the Rock Hill shelves with newspapers and publications from the eighteen hundreds, and his furniture was period-consistent. The wheel turns.

When we left Ann Arbor, we sold or gave away thousands of books; we sold or donated chairs and tables and the accumulated incidentals of our thirty-year residence on Concord Road. But there were items—family furniture and cutlery and paintings—with which we could not part. So we did what many Americans do, whether poor or middle-class or wealthy, and rented storage units. We filled three of them with objects that were the containers of memory and postponed a decision as to disposal; we'd get around to it, we told each other, when the time was ripe.

Two days before we planned to leave, Elena noticed an ad for a condominium for sale, in a development called Earhart Village with which we were familiar. On a lark, we drove to see the place and—with proceeds from the sale of our Concord Road house—bought it on the spot. It was a standard-issue two-story residence: three bedrooms, two-and-a-half bathrooms, a living room and kitchen and, across the courtyard, a garage. There are dozens of similar units all painted the same muted brown and with roughly the same floor plan and compact interior space. The "village" boasts a landscaped uniformity, a common clubhouse with a swimming pool kept open during the summer. Its maintenance crew repairs the roofs and gutters, plows and salts the roadways, and trims the trees and grass and shrubs. Though each of the six houses I earlier described were, to a greater or lesser degree, "one of a kind," there's a purposive anonymity to these structures standing cheek by jowl; it's only by the number at the doorway that you know you've arrived at your home.

We emptied out the storage bins and slept, again, in our old beds and sat on our old chairs. We needed to buy neither coffee cups nor plates nor forks and knives; we needed only to unpack the boxes packed for storage and were *chez nous* again. The art and photographs hung on new walls; the rugs festooned new floors. But it was all the same "surround": a constancy in change.

What's the moral here? Are we like hermit crabs or fiddler crabs or those horseshoe crabs that litter the shores of Cape Cod? Shellfish have a chitinous exoskeleton and, as they molt and grow larger, they leave the once-protective carapace behind. They shift their coloration also; a baby horseshoe crab—no larger than a fingernail—is nearly translucent. The young ones are colored light yellow, the foot-long elders, a dark brown. One determines the age of a tree by counting its internal rings, but a crab or lobster's age corresponds to the number of times it has grown to inhabit an ever-more-sizeable shell. How often it molts is how large it becomes; a "chicken" lobster weighs one pound, but a three pounder has shed its exoskeleton repeatedly and grown to fill the new frame. Shape and proportions remain.

A tree is shallow or deep rooted; a crab and a lobster roam. We human animals don't carry houses with us when we wander, and the transformational tales of America—think of the president born in a log cabin or the financier confined to a jail-cell—suggest homes may be mutable as well as various. It's possible to change both their size and locale. (I'm not referring here to mobile homes or campers, those purposively transient shelters on the open road.) The American Dream is one of expansion requiring an ever-larger container; yet the thing contained stays the same. What surrounds us is our future and that shape-shifter, the past.

To this list of seven houses I need to add three apartments, though we don't technically own the one in which we these days reside. Rather, we own shares in a cooperative venture, and the rules that govern co-ops in New York City are rigid. You have to jump through hoops to gain entry to a building and, once accepted as an occupant, you can't repaint the hall. It's a very different kind of ownership than that which obtained in Spraguetown Road, where I could cheerfully demolish what had been there before. Here the roof is the responsibility of the corporation; here the boiler in the basement is not mine to repair.

Our first such apartment, on 285 Riverside Drive, was one Elena owned when we married in 1970. She had bought it for a song. Though an excellent place to inhabit alone, and with the protection of doormen, it did not serve us well as a shared space. The single bedroom gave out on an alley; the plumbing was ancient, the plaster peeling, and the windows gray. It was an expendable part of what had been a many-roomed residence, divided up when the building went "co-op" in order to increase the number of units for sale. I used to get my daily exercise by opening the window and, after an acrobatic torso-twisting maneuver, look up to see the sky and weather, trying to find clouds or sun.

The maintenance, back then, was seventy-three dollars per month. This seemed to me outrageously high, and I persuaded my new bride—the more fool me!—to sell. We left New York and lived on the farm and then in the sequence of homes here described. Ten years ago, in the same neighborhood, we bought a pied-à-terre a few streets away, and stayed there some months a year. High-ceilinged and large-windowed, the three rooms of our apartment were a retired couple's nest-egg nest, and if I scant the description here it's because these domiciles don't fit a pattern of ownership beneath a private roof.

In the month of my eightieth birthday, we increased our footprint by purchasing a larger apartment in a larger building, still in the same neighborhood and fronting Riverside Drive. We believe—though all such plans must be provisional—this will be our last Manhattan address. It isn't home but is a great gift, a chance to revel in the metropolis with its non-stop spectacle, its cornucopia of cultural events, its occupations and pre-occupations. New York plays the perfect counterpoint to the melody of Cape Cod: the cars not geese that honk, the rumble and tumble of traffic not surf. Every morning when I wake and every night getting ready for sleep, I stare at the trees and the Hudson River and the Palisades beyond. I watch the planes and boats glide past, those emblems of purposive travel, and am thankful finally to have no need or desire to board them. The sunsets are astonishing, and sunrise gets reflected in the windows of Fort Lee.

Another text could be written on the kind of neighborhood apartment buildings offer, or what it means to have a "super" living down below. More people inhabit this single structure on

Riverside Drive than occupied the streets I lived in over the last fifty years. I know my neighbors' names, if at all, because of the building directory; the elevator is more welcome when empty than full.

But sometimes, smiling wordlessly at a child with backpack heading off to school, a man with a briefcase departing for work, an old woman with a shopping cart who labors down the hall, I find myself remembering that child and boy and man who slept elsewhere beneath his several roofs. The houses have a timeline tied to them; they signal stages of age. Food and clothing may sustain or cover us; shelter can do both.

The catchall genre we call autobiography has, it seems to me, several forms. Of the various subsets, let me list a few. This is neither an exhaustive list nor one arranged in order of importance, but it does cover some ground. My phrase *it seems to me* is implicit for each author and has in the twenty-first century grown explicit. The terrain we pass through shows our footprints, first to last.

There are inadvertent autobiographies, or those not conceived of as such. These include diary entries, letters, journals, commonplace books. Years after the date of composition, the writer (or some someone who honors them) retrieves these parts and makes of them a whole. An exchange of love letters, composed with only one reader in mind, becomes a record of courtship or marriage perused by total strangers. There are trip logs, in which the wanderer keeps a daily list of sights or animals or tribes encountered. Written in the moment and not as retrospect, they provide a record of time passing once the time has passed.

Such pages compiled without conscious intent can become a historical record. Years later—and, usually, postmortem—the life of the author comes clear. We who read such records long after the fact have the advantage of perspective, knowing the end of the story though the tale-teller does not. We understand more about Anne Frank's situation than she intended others to learn; we know more about Charles Darwin than he planned to reveal.

This is not always the case. Casanova's voluminous memoirs or the diaries of Samuel Pepys may not have had fame as a principal aim, but there's an outward-facing aspect to their inward-facing gaze. *The Diaries of Anais Nin* (begun when she was eleven years old) were written with at least some sense that somebody else would peruse them. Such confessional texts are often published posthumously, when the writer's dirty linen can be aired.

The reverse is also true. Some books are meant to shock, and publication was all along part of the plan. One version of this category is "My Secret Life." Frank Harris wrote the four-volume *My Life and Loves* (1922–1927), with a hoped-for and soon-realized readership. His suggestive title has spawned an industry. Such titles as *My Secret Life as an American Teenager, My Secret Life on the McJob, My Secret Life on the Dating App Inferno* are commonplace today. A "secret" proclaimed on the cover means something has been printed and revealed.

In any case such airing—as Hamlet puts it, the desire to "tell my story right"—is central to the genre. The privately published scrapbook, by which a patriarch or matriarch leaves markers for the family, has become a thriving industry. The memoir—or *me*moir—abounds. One could argue, indeed, that autobiography is the dominant form of tale-telling in our present moment; personal journalism and the first-person essay have come to claim the field. The platform of the internet has given democratic license to all who wish to "post." Facebook, Snapchat, Instagram, X and the rest are newly available ways of fashioning an at-least-momentary entry in the record of the self.

But autobiography is a long-established, not new, mode. Consider Michel de Montaigne (1533–1592), who spent years in seclusion, composing the *Essais.* His meditations are widely construed to be the first major examples of self-reflexive study on how to live a life. Although he wrote them for his own private pleasure and instruction, it was also true that he hoped his precepts on behavior would thereafter be shared; the confessional mode anticipates a second set of eyes. All such accounts—from St. Augustine's *Confessions* in the fourth century to Alix Kate Shulman's *Memoirs of an Ex-Prom Queen* (1972) and the spate of present-day sensational disclosures—require that some other someone pay attention.

Indeed, it's almost a sine qua non of the genre: A tree fallen in the forest where there's no one near to hear it makes, it has been argued, no real sound. *The Autobiography of Benjamin Franklin* (1793), although published in France two years earlier, had its author's native audience very much in mind. We hope to be exemplary as well as one of a kind.

In his *Cape Cod* (1865), Henry David Thoreau describes a Wellfleet oysterman standing by the fireplace while telling tales. Thoreau in his exploratory ramble had stopped at the oysterman's cottage and recorded an encounter with the man who made him and his fellow traveler welcome. ("This was the merriest old man that we had ever seen, and one of the best preserved. His style of conversation was coarse and plain enough to have suited Rabelais.") It's the fifth chapter in the book, full of anecdote and observation: local lore and food and attitude and scenery. The guest describes his talkative host:

> He remembered well General Washington, and how he rode his horse along the streets of Boston, and he stood up to show us how he looked. "He was a r-a-ther large and portly-looking man, a manly and resolute-looking officer, with a pretty good leg as he sat on his horse. There, I'll tell you, this was the way with Washington." Then he jumped up again, and bowed gracefully to right and left, making show as if he were waving his hat. Said he, "That was Washington."

I know the house—still standing—where John Newcomb regaled his visitors, and know the fireplace in front of which he stood both in fact and on the page. The house, hidden in the Wellfleet woods, is an eighteenth-century structure updated but not much changed. The descendants of old Newcomb—who gave his name to a nearby beach—still live in the village today. But whether the old oysterman actually rolled up his pants to show a "pretty good leg" or just in Thoreau's account of a visit is anybody's guess.

Such inventiveness holds true for travel writing of the little or large sort. "Dr. Livingstone, I presume," is the famous sentence uttered on November 10, 1871, by the journalist Henry Stanley. In the middle of a continent, and after a long and arduous search, he caught up with Dr. David Livingstone in the settlement of Ujii on the shores of Lake Tanganyika. *How I Found Livingstone in Central Africa,* by Henry Morton Stanley, made its author a celebrity, and his travel narrative can still be read today. But whether in fact Stanley uttered those lines at the meeting or embroidered them for publication is beyond any reader's knowledge. In some sense it doesn't matter, just as it doesn't matter if Cortez (in Keats's "On First Looking into Chapman's Homer") gazed from an accurately located "peak in Darien," or if Shakespeare mistakenly gave landlocked Bohemia a seacoast.

The vivid recounting is all.

Long years ago, Elena and I stood in the airport at Colombo, hoping for a plane to carry us away. The airport tarmac, the evening we landed, had been surrounded by tanks. It was in the spring of 1971, a time of national upheaval; Ceylon was becoming Sri Lanka, and travel curfews were being imposed.

Our experience of Ceylon/Sri Lanka had been brief. The first night or two we stayed in the Galle Face Hotel in the center of town, but management urged us to leave. Then we were held in virtual seclusion, though scarcely under duress, at the Mount Lavinia Hotel some distance outside of Colombo. No one in authority could say when the curfew would be lifted. Hill stations had been overrun, and the conflict with the Tamil Tigers was exploding; our plan to travel up to Kandy and explore the countryside would need to be deferred.

After some days we took an offer of evacuation and bade farewell to a country we had intended to visit at length. The capital city was in lockdown, and it seemed sensible—after a week of forced inaction—to "escape."

I put the word in quotes because I never had the slightest sense of personal risk or danger. Out of our hotel window we saw trainloads of workers making for town and then, at dusk, returning. We heard what might have been a rifle or two, or a car engine backfiring, and that was that. We were on our honeymoon, and everything was new to us: the multicolored birds, the tropical luxuriance of the hotel gardens, the placard in our room that read—I transcribe it verbatim—"Beyond eleven o'clock the honorable guest is pried not to disturb the night's still of other honorable guest!"

Our itinerary—those were the days of tickets stapled together in sequence—had us departing Colombo for, if memory serves, Bangkok. But the only flight leaving—and the only one we were permitted to board—was instead bound for Singapore. "Blown off course," we took the plane. When our almost-empty carrier reached that distant destination, there were reporters waiting. I left my bride to deal with them and hurried to an airport phone in order to secure accommodation at the Raffles Hotel. We had prebooked a stay in that fabled sanctuary, but it was scheduled a month thence, and I asked the concierge if possibly they had a room. I was a writer, I explained, and greatly admired Somerset Maugham, and though I was certain the Raffles was full I hoped there might be something suddenly available. If, perhaps, they had a cancellation and could take us in . . .

The man at the desk said, "Yes."

I said, "Oh good" and repeated that our visit was unplanned. Or, rather, that it had been planned for the following month, but we were unexpectedly early since our route had changed.

"Where are you coming from, sir?"

"Colombo."

He assured me there was space and, not to worry, we would be made welcome.

I went back to the airplane to retrieve my wife; she was still talking to cameramen and reporters. She is photogenic and, as the men dispersed, I asked her what she told them.

"Nothing," said Elena. "They wanted to know if I'd seen violence. I said, 'No.'"

"Gunshots? Did they talk about any gunshots?"

"I said we weren't sure they were gunshots."

"Did they ask if we were hostages?"

"Yes. And I said, 'No.'"

We arrived at the Raffles Hotel. Though it has since been reconstructed and much modernized, it was then in what can kindly be called a condition of desuetude; the palm court had been neither swept nor sluiced, the chairs were rickety, the tables required repair. Whole floors were closed, and there were very few guests and many empty rooms. Dogs lay on the cracked patio tiles; birds defecated in the branches of ill-tended trees. We ordered a pair of Singapore Slings and some sort of noodle dish; it had been a lengthy if dull journey and an uneventful day. We slept the sleep of the just.

Next morning *The Straits Times* of Singapore arrived at our door, and there was a photograph of Elena on the airplane exit ramp together with the headline: "Tourists Being Told to leave Ceylon." In less-than-perfect English, the article proclaimed that "an American housewife"—her name spelled out but misspelled—had witnessed hand-to-hand combat and government sharpshooters and prison vans and general confusion in the streets. Forty-four hill stations had been overrun by rebels, and there was pandemonium and an uncertain future for the government of Sirimavo Bandaranaike, recently established and already at great risk. The Sri Lanka Freedom Party and its first female prime minister had been severely tested, the reporter claimed, and the American hostage and her husband had barely escaped with their lives. They thanked their lucky stars they had arrived in Singapore and looked forward to their stay.

What to make of this in hindsight and half the world away? The photograph was accurate, the story a fabrication, yet the two together comprise an "eyewitness account." In some degree this seems to me the way all travel tales are manufactured, whether those of Prester John or Marco Polo, or the travails of newlyweds in a distant place. The actual newspaper article lies moldering in a cardboard box in our attic; the memory of our stay in what soon would be called Sri Lanka grows dim. Yet I find myself mapping the distance between what happened in flat fact and the embroidered account.

Here's the first paragraph from *The Straits Times* of April 9, 1971. "An American housewife, Mrs. Eleana Delbanci [*sic*], who flew into Singapore from Colombo by Air Ceylon tonight said that she learnt that there was much bloodshed in the island . . . all tourists like the local people were kept away from the streets by the curfew. . . . She also heard that students were fighting the armed forces and the police."

The story was a function of imagination, not reportage—what we now label "fake news." And though the anecdote of our departure from what is now known as Bandaranaike Airport is—to the best of my memory—correct, the passage of time has done its slow work and touched up the narrative. Perhaps it's more exact to say that any such account is a refashioning of the raw stuff of experience into something shapely. It's a blend of fact and fiction, a journey recorded long after the fact and not, as it were, "on the road." In the far reach of recollection, the dialogue I offered up earlier ("Nothing," said Elena. "They wanted to know if I'd seen violence . . . ") is accurate, but it is of course reconstituted conversation and not a transcription thereof. All travel writing—except for unedited excerpts from a wanderer's journal or ship's log—partakes of just such revision: (e)motion recollected in tranquility and at the writing desk.

"The prime of life" is an elastic category, since goal posts keep being moved. Actuarial tables shift. Not all that long ago the average life expectancy of our species, Homo sapiens, was half the length it is today, and therefore "middle age" must be a variable number and term.

From such all-leveling disasters as war or pestilence, no one is exempt. And I know of no useful distinction between the lifespan of creative artists and that of the public writ large. So it's fair to assume that professional painters, musicians, and writers submit to the "whirligig of time"— Shakespeare's phrase for the passage of years—in the same way and with the same statistical results as do men and women engaged in other fields.

Here too the clock ticks and tocks. The dating of Shakespeare's sonnets is less than firmly established (as is the date of his birth), but when he penned his self-reflexive description of physical collapse—"That time of year thou may'st in me behold"—he was perhaps thirty-four. In Sonnet 73 the speaker/writer declares, "In me thou see'st the twilight of such day / As after sunset fadeth in the west," and though poetic license and hyperbole are here involved, the first-person pronoun is telling. At his death in 1616 he was a little past fifty; in terms of modern expectation, the Bard of Avon died more than a decade earlier than our present retirement age.

In the Pleistocene Epoch most members of a clan were dead by thirty, and only a very few, it seems, reached the outer limit of fifty. Women—because of the dangers of childbearing—routinely died younger than men; the reverse is now the case. In the Roman Empire, the average life expectancy is thought to have been twenty-eight; as recently as 1900, the number was forty-five. The French used to call the *troisième age*, or "third age," that time of life which starts at sixty, and the implicit understanding was that sixty heralded the end of the performance. There would be no fourth act.

In *The Education of Henry Adams,* the writer refers to himself in the third person. Let me try that device on for size:

Nicholas Delbanco has written two book-ended books. The first dealt with artists past the age of seventy: *Lastingness: The Art of Old Age* (2011). Paradoxically, perhaps, and against the logic of chronology, the second of these studies came out two years thereafter. Its title was *The Art of Youth: Crane, Carrington, Gershwin, and the Nature of First Acts* (2013).

The former described a series of creative men and women who maintained their productivity in older age; the latter studied those who were extinguished early. Between the author's cut-off point for "first acts"—the age of forty—and the starting point for "lastingness," there stretches the thirty-year interval we label middle age. And though his thoughts will constitute neither a book-length nor a research project, he wants to consider that interval, sometimes called "the prime of life."

Enough of that. The rhetorical strategy of the third person won't wash. Change "*he wants* to consider that interval" to "*I want* to consider that interval" and we're closer to the mark. It's "me, myself, and I" who has "authorized" these meditations, not some impersonal someone who happens to have the same name. As I approach the end of life, I'm more and more aware of how I used to feel and things I used to want that I no longer want or feel: A graceful death means more to me than it did in youth or middle age.

Indeed, the situation of *Still Life at Eighty* seems related to the way we deal with some other someone's soon-approaching death. With luck, the passing on is almost imperceptible, the loss of a loved one prepared for and with few regrets. There's melancholy, yes, but also a sense of time well spent. The burial procedures both comfort and distract us. We go about our occupations as though they were important, or at least absorbing, and are surprised by grief. A memory unbidden, a sight or smell or taste recalled, a gesture repeated: All these seem unavoidable as well as preordained. Too, there's consolation in survival: *There, but for the grace of God, went I. . . .*

For this author—and, I suspect, for many others—the second act seemed less compelling than the first and third. Raphael died well before forty, Michelangelo at nearly ninety. Who knows what would have happened had their lifespans been reversed? My imagination could be fired by the dead-too-soon Giorgione or the nonagenarian Titian, but those adult artists who labored through the intervening time looked merely dutiful. From forty to sixty may be our most productive period, but romance attaches to the previous and melancholy to the later years; it's not, I think, an accident that our heroines and heroes by and large expire young. The pup and the old dog are the subjects of our stories, not the grown-up in between.

Or so it seemed. But now—to quote Macbeth—my season is "the sere, the yellow leaf," and I look back on the middle years with incremental interest. What were the occupations—the *pre*-occupations—of that fellow who went busily to work, who woke each morning with a sense of what the day would bring that might prove new and different, or continue much the same? His ambitions, expectations, and desires now seem both distant and dim. And I think it worth pondering what it signifies, in terms of first and final acts, to have been "between."

Or, perhaps, "betwixt." Less common in usage, and archaic if not yet obsolete, the word derives from the Old English *betweox* and the Middle English *bitwixe,* meaning something positioned more or less equidistant from two separated objects or conditions. To take just a pair of examples: In the nursery rhyme we learned as children, "Jack Sprat could eat no fat / His wife could eat no lean / And so betwixt the two of them / They licked the platter clean." In a second instance, the lower spar on a sailing ship—which needed to be scrubbed clean of slime, but would be wave-battered—was called "the devil spar." The poor sailor hoisted overboard to do a morning's dirty work was, in the old expression, "betwixt the devil and the deep blue sea."

To my ear, at any rate, the word *betwixt* is more closely connected to its adjacent objects than the expansive *between*; it claims a kinship with surrounding entities, a nearer relation to what went before and what follows after. We're between romantic partners or jobs, but betwixt a rock and a hard place. Mostly, the two mean the same, and both describe indeterminacy: a soft connective tissue for like or dissimilar things.

The shift from year to year in a young child is notable; "between" the ages of two and five a chasm yawns, and an explosion of growth. The reverse can be the case for the nonagenarian; a decline between the ages of, say, ninety-two and ninety-five may be steep. But the forties and the fifties tend to blur, at least in memory; there's such a rush and bustle about the procedures of the workaday world that it sometimes seems useless to date with precision the turning point as *here,* not *there*; did the pivotal moment come *then*?

"The middle distance" is defined in art as a pictorial representation of space "betwixt" the foreground and the background of a composition. In track, horse racing, swimming, cross-country skiing, and other sports, it's the extent of a contest "between" the short and the marathon race.

We tend to honor compromise, a position taken between two extremes; but in Soviet usage, or so I'm told, the noun for *compromise* was inalienably associated with the adjective for *putrid.* To be betwixt the young and old is to partake of both but be neither, and the waves that will wash over you while scrubbing the spar free of barnacles may be both salt and chill. You keep your head down and keep scraping, and keep scraping by . . .

Elena and I drove, recently, to a meeting up in Riverdale about a prospective "retirement home." North of Manhattan, and fronting the Hudson River, the structure has yet to be built. They call it a managed care facility, still in the planning stage, and none of this felt urgent. But my wife has a habit of planning ahead and wants to make certain we won't die in need, so it seemed sensible to think about the prospect of a move, some years hence, into a place where the health care is at hand and guaranteed. Her parents had both died at home, but home was thirty miles from the nearest, and second-rate, hospital; in their final years they were attended to by a series of local women, whose skills were less than confidence-inspiring. For Elena, her parents' plight was a cautionary tale: Their long lingering decline had been both expensive and sad.

Therefore we thought we'd take a look at what was on offer in the brochure for "River's Edge" and see if it might be the place we move to next. In *Lastingness: The Art of Old Age*, my thesis was (and is) that there's a cadre of creative individuals who at least maintain and in some cases advance their art towards the end—think of Titian, Verdi, Yeats. As something of an expert on the "business" of growing old, and in the course of promoting the book, I visited a series of retirement communities.

To put it bluntly, there were differences between them. They ranged from the dispiriting to the enlivening, the execrable to the excellent. There's a kind of checklist—the degree of independence offered, the degree of privacy, religious affiliation, the number and quality of staff, the variety of restaurants, the size of the swimming pool, the availability of studio space, the proximity to doctors—that defines an institution and, in this context, its rank. I'm not discussing nursing homes or "assisted living" facilities, which are functional at best. Managed care is a competitive growth industry, since our population is aging, and retired "baby boomers" have as-yet-unmet needs.

There are Quaker retreats, Zen-influenced retreats, retreats for those whose minds and bodies are failing or have failed. There are cradle-to-grave establishments, if the cradle be defined as something that starts rocking at, say, sixty-five. My stepmother, recently dead at one hundred-and-two, lived for many years in one such facility in Roland Park in Baltimore. By any checklist the place is first-rate, but the view from her windows was less than lovely, whereas River's Edge in Riverdale overlooks the beautiful Hudson and the Palisades. It would be in hailing distance for our family and friends, and as long as we were mobile we'd have access to the city . . .

I went to school not far away and knew the neighborhood's streets. Security guards waved us in. There was sculpture on the lawns and a nearby mansion called "Wave Hill" where the great conductor Arturo Toscanini lived and died. The famed and long-established Hebrew Home for the Aged stood on an adjacent lot. We were offered name tags and a plastic bottle of water and urged to step inside. The structure to which we were conducted was soon to be torn down and replaced by the new building. The walls were lined with photographs of happy, well-fed couples on a picnic or admiring a flower arrangement or walking a leashed dog. The eleven o'clock "Welcome to River's Edge" presentation was already underway. Soon, they would serve lunch.

First came a talk about the logic of preparing for a protected old age and managed care and the financial advantages of planning in advance. The crowd of prospective clients was escorted by four women in their fifties—making small talk, making promises, making sure that each potential customer felt singled out. There were roughly thirty of us: slow or spry, talkative or silent, white or brown or black.

"We strive for diversity," one of the agents said.

Our common denominator was age and a degree of affluence. Seventy-five is the average age for those who've shown sufficient interest to visit the planned site. The poor can't afford such creature comforts; the truly wealthy finance their own retirement home. The matter of income and fiscal resources affects these calculations, but not at this first stage. We were given no actual numbers: the size of a down payment, the cost of an apartment, the monthly maintenance fee . . .

In answer to Elena's question, "It's too soon," the agent said, "We're still putting together the specs. But"—she waved at us, inclusive—"you're in on the ground floor."

I found myself resisting the spiel, the snake-oil promise of the excellence of what we couldn't see. We were asked to imagine the beauty of top-of-the-line fixtures in a nonexistent bathroom and the appliances as yet unordered for the kitchen nook. We were told we'd learn to like each other and establish a community with others who signed up. "You're all so *interesting*," said the woman. "Trust me. You'll be happy here."

I doubted it. Still, we put down a deposit (minimal, refundable with interest) in order to stay in the loop. The project is as yet notional, its actuality distant, and this permitted me to persevere in the habit of delay. Deferral is the chosen mode for those of us who don't look in the mirror or gauge the daily number of pills swallowed or trips to the bathroom to empty a bladder. It's a kind of ostrich principle or habit of denial, and so far it's seen me through.

Driving back into the city, I felt both satisfied and desolate: How had we reached this stage? Old people's homes are for old people, not me and my wife, and a principal attraction of the prospect was its distance; we didn't yet need to decide. But, changing lanes, I caught sight of my face in the car's rearview mirror, and—though it's the Hudson, not the Styx—knew myself to be at river's edge.

Each of us has dreams to dream or nightmares to escape from; each one of us rules out—consciously or by inadvertence—alternative ways of being. Decisions must be made. I knew early on, I think, that I would never become a professional basketball player or stock-car racer or concert pianist or dentist, but the future did feel rife with possibility. There were contests to enter, goals to attain, prizes to win. There were girls to hold hands with and, later, have sex with; there were friends to make and walks to take and books to read and, later, write. There was law school to consider, medical school to attend or avoid, business school to apply to or shun.

Everywhere stretched roads not taken, forest paths to follow or leave unexplored. The map of each existence is full of false starts, detours, and reversals, and no individual's journey is a straight unbroken line. Since a straight line is defined as the shortest distance between two points—and if those points are birth and death—only the infant lost in utero will not know those wanderings and vagaries we call the lived life.

All such decision-taking is a matter of self-definition and choice for the fortunate few. A large percentage of the people who attain their middle years do so without options. For the unemployed mechanic or factory worker or farm laborer such challenging alternatives as law or business or medical school are merely notional. It used to be the rule—and in much of the world remains that way—that you do what your parents and grandparents did, and do as you've been told. The subsistence farmer and hunter and gatherer have no such opportunity to choose or to avoid routine; this business of the invented self and elected path is a function of, if not luxury, privilege.

Or, perhaps, necessity. Some folk are forced to change their preset ways and find new lives to live. Some reinvent themselves in exile or as displaced or imprisoned persons; some deal with catastrophic illness or the loss of livelihood and limbs. The sentimental remembrance that "there were contests to enter, goals to attain, prizes to win" is a result of open-ended possibility, not of options foreclosed.

Therefore, I admit to begin with that this discussion of midlife behavior is a subset of the whole. Not all of us can lay claim to autonomy, and often the illusion of choice is just that. It's part of the old argument about free will versus determinism; quite often what we choose to do and think of as our own decision has been preordained.

Let's shift the image, therefore, to one without radical change. Think of the young man or woman astride the hub of a slow-turning wheel, with spokes directed outwards, each in a slightly different direction: The arc of *this* career is two degrees higher or lower than the arc of *that* one, while the wheel revolves. Or think of a game of roulette, where the wheel stops spinning on a number we choose or avoid. Or gamble instead on a color, not number: If we pick *Red* we lose; if we pick the adjacent *Black* we win. These are only approximate models for decisions taken and bets placed; the system of advancement is not always ours to choose.

When it does become a conscious choice, however—as in Frost's "I took the road less traveled by"—it makes "all the difference." To continue with the journey-metaphor, and quote an additional poet, the opening line of Dante's *Commedia* declares "*Nel mezzo del cammin di nostra vita . . .*" (In the middle of the road of our life), we look around and take our bearings and attempt to not be lost. "*Mi ritrovai en una bosca oscura*," the pilgrim writes: "I found myself in a dark wood." He was thirty-five when he wrote this line—or half the then-current extent of the classical three-score and ten years of life. He begins his exploration—of hell and purgatory and, at last, paradise—with a moment of uncertainty before putting foot after foot.

At some point in the process, we follow a governing compass-direction, even if (and sometimes because) it's unclear at the time. The decision to marry or enlist or become a parent or enter into a contractual agreement or join a team or gang or club or congregation means we expand the boundaries of self. The decision to "go it alone" is also a defining one, and only in retrospect do we gain clarity as to a decision's effects. What seemed casual will have been causal; what seemed momentous will, once the moment has passed, be in effect ineffective. That "slow-turning wheel" acquires momentum, and at a certain point we recognize we've gone far down a track.

My life has been a lucky one, and I am daily conscious of my great good fortune. Though born during Hitler's fearsome reign, and in beleaguered London, neither I nor any member of my immediate family were casualties of the Second World War. My parents died of natural causes; I hope to do so as well. My wife is, daily and yearly, a wonder and a gift; our two daughters and their own daughters are too. My health has had its challenges, but at eighty I'm upright and hale. The places I call home are safe and beautiful; the bank declares me solvent and does not bounce my checks. At this age and stage of what's become statistically a lengthy life, what I dream of is more of the same.

Elena and I spent two weeks in Morocco. We visited medinas, the lunar landscape of the Sahara, the snow-capped Atlas Mountains, the ochre-colored villages that blend into brown hills. There's much to write about—the courteous demeanor of our hosts, my tourist's ride on camelback, a bargaining system where it's an insult to pay an item's asking price, the windswept silence of a tent pitched in a white bowl of sand. But because I'm a writer whose medium is language, I want to write about the lack of it instead.

In the world of Islam, it is forbidden to use "graven images" or to display representational art. Photography's permitted, and there are myriad photographs of Mohammed VI, the king of Morocco since 1999. But to my Western eyes, the pattern of script is abstract, not instructional. I mean by this that the verses of the Koran—beautifully inscribed on gates or the walls of Mosques—are not ones I can decipher. The religious iconography we Westerners are used to—stained glass windows, sculpture, murals, triptychs, altarpieces, and so forth—is in part information-transmission, a way of telling a story to those who cannot read. An unlettered worshipper can see the Christ child in a manger or on the road to Calvary or brought down from the Cross. To my untutored eyes, however, the designs on walls in Morocco were not illustrative. I could appreciate the style and symmetry of letters and the elegance of inscription but not what the language conveyed. They meant much to those who could read them but not, alas, to me.

This held true as well of the Berber alphabet, the language of the original travelers to what became known as "the Barbary Coast." The Berber tribes, who crisscrossed the country (and made Jews, then Christians, then Muslims welcome) tell time-honored stories, but not ones I could understand. The French colonized Morocco, and road and shop signs everywhere attested to a lingering French influence. I speak, read, and write both English and French. Yet, for all practical purposes, my wife and I were functionally illiterate as to what these written symbols might mean.

Our guide was patient, generous, but our attempts at intonation and pronunciation of the few words he conveyed to us in Arabic or Berber felt foredoomed to fail. His English was of course up to the task of communication, since English has become the lingua franca or sine qua non—both Latin terms—of the commercial world. The first suggests that the French tongue once was indispensable to international discourse; the second suggests that without English we're nothing now, mere mutes. But what I mostly felt on camelback or in the crowded souk was tongue-tied and inept.

We may "read" the sand or clouds or formations of rock for what they tell of water or weather or the prospect of shelter from storms. We may track hoofprints or the distant green of shrubbery for what they tell us of watering holes and the availability of food. But a sign proclaiming "McDonald's" or "Welcome to Iowa City" requires, of its reader, a different sort of skill. And much of our time in Morocco was spent in the attempt to decipher what was written on the wind and sand, but not upon a page. On an ancient camel route, there was only one sign I could read in its entirety (and in English): "54 days to Timbuktu."

A muezzin calls the faithful to prayer five times daily from a minaret, and worshippers turn toward Mecca and perform their silent devotion on the streets or in a mosque. The rapid exchange between salesman and customer takes place in terms I'm unable to fathom, and the chatter of family members or friends is not for me to hear. When you scrutinize a wavy or an upright line and can make no sense of it you're back to the circumscribed vista of childhood: *What's that? What's this? What does it signify?*

No matter how large the anticipated or actual audience for a book, the act of composition remains a private task. It requires silence and a degree of solitude. Yet when the daily round entails outward-facing labor—as in the classroom or at some sort of podium or editor's desk—it has a different feel, partaking of community and communication. This is the public aspect of English, not the introspective one. Language becomes a function less of private formulation than of public discourse, and for me at least it signals some of what we mean by "getting and spending," the world not too much with us but knocking at the door.

One risk of retirement, often attested to, is the recognition that the world no longer knocks, no longer cares for or defers to our opinion. An at-first-aggrieved and then resigned sense of irrelevance is a common hallmark of those past middle age. And though much of this is delusional, the feeling in the prime of life that what we say or feel or do might matter is a principal yield of the period, a principal return on the investment of attention.

Which is a fancy way of saying that a marker for those decades is the degree to which we feel engaged.

The hurry and bustle prompted by other people's expectations—their expressed approval or dissatisfaction—mark the middle years. Whether in a family or politics or business or military or professional service, the mid-career worker has a time clock to punch, a meeting to join, a meal to prepare, a phone call to take or a delivery make. The sum of these commitments adds up to that sense of engagement that gets us through the day. You are hired or fired, grow rich or stay poor, get married or divorced, are elected or voted out of office, or change your religion or sex. It's a busy time, a fruitful or a fruitless one; but for those of us now in the *troisième age,* it went by in a blur.

For the very elderly, for whom short-term memory fades and proper names get lost or misplaced, the vivid return of (and in some cases to) childhood means that middle age gets relegated to the dustbin of personal history. What emerges clearly are the dreams and desires of youth. It's why first love or your "first time" remain indelible; it's why a childhood insult rankles after sixty years.

Maturity is best defined-in terms of perspective: It is that period when you may take the measure of what went before; you may predict, with a degree of accuracy, what remains to come. And maturity itself is a semi-permeable membrane, an open-ended condition; few can say with certainty, "On such and such a day and for such and such a reason I became mature. . ."

Some "grow old before their time"; others remain "young at heart." We're told to "act your age." But these are expressions of attitude and not based on actuarial statistics. I never thought, when twenty, that I'd be writing this at eighty, and that half the threescore years intervening would constitute what we call the prime of life. Vantage shifts. When young we glance at a forty-year-old and think how very old they seem; when old we see a forty-year-old and say to ourselves, "How young!"

I heard a story, some time back, of a "prophet" in a southern state of India, Kerala. In his farming village, the question of gender in an unborn baby remains a crucial one, since parents hope to have a son and not a costly daughter. He would examine a pregnant woman and pronounce: "You will have a boy." Or, alternatively, "a girl." The seer kept a record of these verdicts and had a reputation for great probity because, if wrong, he uncomplainingly returned the client's fee. In fifty percent of the cases his prophecy was correct. Too, there were some disappointed parents who didn't come back to claim their fee, if the prediction proved inaccurate. As a result, the margin of profit for his business was guaranteed, and high.

This went on for some time. Then a neighboring soothsayer established a competing booth, with one crucial difference. He too pronounced, "a boy" or "a girl," but reversed the gender in his written account of each transaction, and in this fashion the books were cooked. If the prophecy was accurate—which proved, statistically, to be the case half the time—the customer would rest content (or sorrowful) with the result. But if a customer returned to claim a refund, saying, "You promised me a boy, and we have had a girl," the wily merchant would consult his log and say, "No, no, my dear Mrs. Battacharya, you must have misunderstood. See here"—pointing to the inked entry—"it says I said to you, 'Your child will be female, not male.'"

In this way he was proved correct, instead of fifty percent, one-hundred percent of the time. And his profit doubled that of his competitor across the street, and he made a handsome living.

Until, that is, someone discovered the con game and blew the whistle on him and the man was killed.

The moral of this story is that we should refrain from backing up our spoken prophecies with a written record, and doubly so if it's a record of deceit. At some point someone—perhaps with a sharp kris in hand—will hold us to account. Far safer to admit the failure to read tea leaves or lines along an outstretched palm, or the pattern of wet coffee grounds in the bottom of a cup. What we predict or prophesize is at best a guess . . .

My wife is the love of my life. I have put in writing—here and elsewhere—my devotion to Elena. She is the dedicatee of *Still Life at Eighty* and her name concludes this book. As anyone who knows her knows, my wife is a quicksilver creature—so full of talent and attainment that it's hard if not impossible to describe her in a single phrase. For myself, the word "writer" suffices; it's who I've been and what I've done from the start. But Elena is multifaceted; her interests are many and her achievements large.

At the age of seventy, for instance, she conceived and wrote a novel, then published it to loud applause with scarcely a hitch in her stride. *The Silver Swan* (2015) is steeped in the world of classical music, focused on a great cellist, his daughter, and his cello. Grounded in personal experience of that world, it's nonetheless wholly invented as story and is a page-turning read.

Before that, she'd been variously employed, in concert management, in preschool as a kindergarten teacher, in an addiction services agency—Phoenix House—in New York, as a therapist at Bennington in the College Counselling Services, and for a quarter of a century as a faculty member in the Gerald R. Ford School of Public Policy at the University of Michigan. She was my indispensable partner, as these pages will attest, in the writing programs in Vermont and Michigan, which I administered for nearly fifty years. Without her skill at fundraising and her MA in nonprofit management, the Helen Zell Writers Program, with its munificent endowment, might not be enabled today.

But this is a bare-bones summary and should be fleshed out. Elena's ear for music is astonishing; her retention of each note she's heard is "phonographic" in the way that others might possess a photographic memory. Her gifts as a visual artist are real; our walls, and the walls of others, attest to her colorist's eye. Her personal warmth—both social and domestic—is the stuff of local legend. In the words of Isaiah (53:3) she has been "acquainted with grief" and earned compassion shines through. The stranger on the street or in a restaurant or hospital, the house cleaner or hotel worker or ticket taker in a hall—all receive and respond on the instant to her generous attention.

"Love calls us to the things of this world" is a phrase from Pulitzer Prize winner Richard Wilbur's collection, *Things of This World: Poems* (1956). I use that title, here, for Section 3. From the moment I first saw Elena in resplendent youth, at seventeen, to the time we married nine years later, in Vermont, to this early morning's coffee in Massachusetts when we share plans for the day to come, she has been my compass and true north.

My parents and two brothers were and are important to me. Our children and their children are central to the narrative of what has become a shared story, but I won't elaborate here. To do so would be to continue at length in the mode of "I was born on such and such a date to A and B who were married on the afternoon of X in the Town Hall at Y . . ." For that reason I don't name my parents or my brothers; they belong to a different and as-yet-unwritten text. Instead, I want these pages to focus on matters that might matter to other "senior citizens," whose history and circumstance are not the same as mine. The modernist assumption that an artist is inseparable from her or his or our or their art strikes me as open to question; why should *I* mean merely *me?* Why should *mine* stand separate from *yours?*

With luck these pages may prove more than one man's narrative, and the particulars of whom I courted or shook hands with will not take stage center. From a four-foot distance, my hand is mine and mine alone; it tells the noticing witness a good deal about the age and health and strength and race and gender and occupation of the person whose hand it is: his status and statistics. If I hold that palm to my nose, however, and stare at it from a two-inch remove, the hand is Everyman's and the pronoun is *We.*

Still Life at Eighty follows no strict chronological order, from youth to middle to old age; the progress is jagged and fitful. I take one step forward, two back. As is the case with memory, the past and present fuse—and I've made no effort, here, to render sequential the passage of time. A granddaughter may be six or three, the Delta, Omicron, Eris, or emerging version of the coronavirus may have appeared or not as yet been identified, a friend may be dead or alive.

Instead, these pages focus turn by turn on topics that compel me, both in retrospect and prospect. This is, I suppose, as good a working definition of autobiography as any other. An author's writing signals identity; we leave our fingerprints all over every page. No matter how we throw our voice or accent, it comes from the same single throat. "Mirror, mirror on the wall" remains both the opening gambit and the central question here. "Who is the fairest of them all?" becomes a query not about beauty but rightness, balance, probity, as in other meanings of "fair."

Whatever else is true of these pages, I hope that I'll be fair.

PART II

On Churchill's Chair

I have in front of me a black, spring-loaded binder titled ART. A smaller version of the title has been pasted on the spine. The sturdy pebbled folder measures 11½ by 9½ inches, and the whole is an inch thick. Inside are fifty-two pages (one for each week of the year, though I doubt this was intentional) of yellowing foolscap: typed pages with glued on photographs and postcards from the history of painting. Its author signed himself proudly, Nicholas F. Delbanco—in an upward-rising scrawl of black ink—and his chosen title is: THE STORY OF PAINTING FROM CAVE ART TO MODERN TIMES.*

Elsewhere, I called myself "Nicky." I was eleven years old. The dedication page reads:

To my Father
For his kind help
and encouragement that
he gave me throughout my book

On the next page there's a more expansive prefatory acknowledgment: "I would like to thank my father for his help in supplying material and helping me learn my subject. To my mother for her kind encouragement and faith in my book. To my uncle, an art specialist, for his talks to me and helping assemble my book. To my teacher, Mrs. Landis, for her helping arrange my book. To my elder cousin, for his encouragement. To all these people and many more for their very kind and heartening help.

"NICKY DELBANCO"

I'm struck by the term "my subject," and the threefold iteration of "my book," then the earnest thanks for "kind and heartening help." The author was, it seems, precocious as well as pretentious; his table of contents reads:

Preface

1. How Painting Started
2. Art in the Middle Ages
3. The Beginning of the Renaissance
4. The High Renaissance
5. Leonardo Da Vinci
6. Michelangelo and Raphael
7. The Triumph of Light
8. Towards Revolution
9. A New Breed of Artists
10. Painting in our own Time.

That prefatory page concludes, in emulation of works cited in the volume's Bibliography, "Copyright 1954. First Edition."

Most of the photographs and postcards would have come from my father's collection; in his studio he kept a box of small-scale reproductions of prized pictorial art. Sometimes I traced a figure—a stone-age bison or head by Jan Van Eyck—in pencil on the page. The typing is careful, precise. I used my mother's Smith Corona, with its elite twelve-point type. On the relatively few occasions when I made a spelling mistake—this was before the era of "whiteout" or spellcheck —I corrected the errors by hand. Once or twice (as in "faze" for "phase") a spelling error persists. Our author failed to include a "List of Illustrations," but pasted in forty or more. The glue must have been high quality, for the pictures remain attached.

There was, of course, a limit to what I knew and could report; my description of Leonardo's *Mona Lisa*, for example, reads in its entirety: "This was one of his greatest, if not his greatest, works of art." But here's a more characteristic paragraph: "Another Italian painter, Simone Martini, spent some time in Northern Europe. He showed them the new Italian art and the French in turn told him about their Gothic style. Finally the two arts mixed together and a style affectionately called 'International Gothic' developed."

The overall effect is studious and serious—almost comically so, in retrospect—and it's hard not to read with a smile. The writer struck the pose of a dispassionate historian and scholar, describing the work of Gainsborough and Giorgione, of Hals and Hobbema, some fifty named painters in all. And there's a through-line to his inquiry: Who were the great ones and how were they great and why do they matter today?

This "greatest hits" aspect of the essay is hard to ignore. An urge to generalize runs through the text; a desire to make lists and rank practitioners was strong. ART is filled with such pronouncements as: "Nevertheless, the seventeenth century was one of the most important milestones in the history of art. Truly, it was the triumph of light!" Or, of the eighteenth century, "From an artistic point of view England had hardly been looked upon as a leader. But now it began to develop artists—and many good ones—too."

Why, I wonder, did I embark on this project; was it conceived of for school? I have only the most distant memory of "Mrs. Landis," who was my seventh-grade teacher and perhaps suggested a research assignment; she would no doubt have been nonplussed by what young Nicky produced. Industrious, even indefatigable, our author tracked—as in one of the works cited in his bibliography—"The History of Painting." Once the school year finished, I turned twelve years old.

Of my father's amateur interest in making art, and my uncle's professional expertise, I will have more to write later; of my "elder cousin's" help, I can remember nothing, though he might have provided a postcard or three. What strikes me, these many years after the fact, is the self-assurance of the fledgling critic; he concludes his Preface with such generalities as "People sometimes see different things in the same patterns." And "The word 'imagine' means to make an image or a picture in your mind." Then, finally, "I am sure as you read through this book that you will realize the immensity and greatness of the people who helped painting become a great source of joy to countless millions."

It has taken me a goodly while to again "read through this book." And though its author's imagined audience was notional at best, "my book," in its first and only edition, has lasted just short of seventy years. So I find myself remembering that ambitious child who was "sure . . . you (would) read," and his desire to instruct a waiting world as to the glories of "painting . . . a great source of joy." Where did he come from and how did he know what he knew?

Here's a representative paragraph from his discussion of cave art:

> What were these pictures for? They could have been meant to help the hunter, because some of the pictures have spears sticking into the imaginary animal. Perhaps the caveman threw stones at his masterpiece. There could also have been a spiritual meaning behind the paintings. No one will ever know for sure. A good interpretation however is that the man thought if he killed the image of the animal first, he would have no trouble slaughtering the real thing.

In the years since, I've visited such sites as Lascaux and Altamira, and I'm not certain I can improve upon that statement: "No one will ever know for sure." The language of informed inquiry is of course more scholarly than the above, but the kid got it more or less right. He writes about the hungry hunter, immured in walls and on the point of starvation. "At such times he would frequently think of meat and if he finally clubbed a buffalo in his joy he might paint a picture of the beast. Since the men lived in a cave and the cave walls were usually rough, the picture would probably follow an outline of bumps on the surface of the cave."

I am neither editing nor eliding this; it's exactly the language he used. *He* being *I,* a quiet inward-facing boy who had recently been diagnosed with rheumatic fever and spent long months in bed. His governing assumption, here, is that art might "hold a mirror up to nature" and be by it enlivened.

Too, it allowed him/me to pronounce on history. The text is shot through with such passages as:

> The colonies were now old enough to have their own artists. The two most famous of these painters were called Benjamin West and John Singleton Copley. These men, however, did not stay in America long enough to participate in the Revolution. They returned to their mother country to do some exhibiting. These men had such success in London that they stayed there for good. West became extremely famous and was elected president of the British academy of painting. This was somewhat like the French academy but was a lot less severe.

> By now the dream of Napoleon had expired. Gone was the Roman influence. Artists did different paintings and used different techniques. The subject of this painting by Delacroix is "The Abduction of Rebecca." (A full-page black and white reproduction of that oil has been

> glued to the subsequent sheet.) His picture, surprisingly enough, has much the same style as that of Dürer. There are wide flowing brush strokes and a lot of movement. Truly, it is an excellent picture.

How did I gather such information; what judgments was I so complacently making, and value-system expressing? Our would-be Kenneth Clark or Bernard Berenson felt confident, or so it seems, of his aesthetic opinions, by and large approbatory. He didn't bother with work he disliked, or art that failed to impress him; the governing note of his discourse is the note of praise. Advancing from Giotto to Matisse, reporting on their several "ways of seeing"—to borrow John Berger's excellent phrase—he ruminated on style.

At this remove it's hard for me to enter into his eleven-year-old head or heart, but I think his pronouncements had something to do with a desire to join in long-standing tradition, to claim a present part in the history of painting. If you can trace your human ancestry to men using hand-sharpened chisels, or coloring rock with upraised palms, why not assume that art has always been consequential and should be revered? To this present witness, it's more than a little surprising that the not-yet-adolescent was so steadfast in his faith. What intrigues me is his confidence, his wish to offer opinions—though god knows how he/I came by them. To wit:

> Raphael then worked for a long time in Rome redecorating royal buildings. He there did a tremendous amount of Frescoes. While in Rome, he also did some

> architectural work. This was rather unusual for him so he went back to his great pallet [*sic*] and easel.
>
> In Venice Mannerism wasn't so popular but by 1550 it was firmly established. It showed very well in the works of the greatest Venetian Master since Titian. This man's name was Tintoretto. He was truly one of the world's finest artists. This man used quick short strokes of the brush and created quite an effect. Here is one of his best pictures.

Then I pasted in an illustration of Tintoretto's *Miracle of St. Mark* and proceeded to the work of Leonardo (of whose oils and drawings there are three examples). All these decades later the postcards and the photographs adhere to the page; it's a family album of sorts. The pencil sketches and typed notations mark both place and time. And though the prefatory note is personal, the text reads like an effort, now, of impersonal reclamation—or even restoration. Above it hover the spirits of my dead father, my long-dead mother and uncle; from it emanates the odor of my childhood home.

That home had much art on the walls. As I have written elsewhere (in an essay titled "A Visit to the Gallery"), and in an adult's voice:

> Other children spent time with their fathers playing baseball or fishing or working on cars. I spent Saturday morn-

> ings at his side, painting or sitting for portraits, because he was a more than Sunday painter and an accomplished one. Several of his portraits are in fact in public places—the National Portrait Gallery, Harvard College, the Museum of the City of New York. He never quite had the daring or drive to make a career of it and was a collector more than a creator. But he had genuine talent and did love to draw and, in his great old age, declared, "A painting a day keeps the doctor away." When he came home from business trips, it was always with something acquired en route: a Zuni Bowl or hermaphroditic standing figure with breasts and penis I'd stare at in wonder, an etching by Rembrandt or woodcut by Dürer or poster by his favorite, Henri de Toulouse-Lautrec. Lautrec's Aristide Bruant turned his broad back above my childhood bed; Yvette Guilbert smiled soulfully down; La Goulue lifted her leg. There were oil paintings in the dining room by Lovis Corinth and Chagall. And always, when we traveled, it was to the museum or the monastery or the chapel on the edge of town my father took us first.

Tellingly, and for the only two times I used the first-person plural in ART:

> We have a painting by Marc Chagall in our house. He strikes you as if he is in a dream, like he's in a dream world. And truly he is. It is a very hard job to be able to tell what things look like in your inner eye. But Chagall has done it.

And:

> The artists of this time, strangely enough, began not to paint pictures of great favorites but to portray poor laborers. The leader of these artists was a man called Gustave Courbet. (We have a Courbet at home and my impression of his painting is this.) Courbet thought a lot like the old Master, Caravaggio. He was not so interested in painting scenes unless they were scenes which could be happening. Courbet really gave a wonderful depth to his pictures and made you feel like you were watching the very scene.

We did in fact have a Courbet at home—a somewhat dull sylvan landscape hanging opposite my seat at the dining room table; my elder brother got to look at a plate of oysters by Lovis Corinth. For a while there was a naked torso, also, of a woman sculpted by Rodin, but when our mother caught me staring at the statue's breasts too fixedly she made our father dispose of the lady on the pedestal. He exchanged it for a set of six small naked dancers, whose thumbed protuberances (the sculptor first worked his bronzes in clay, then plaster) failed to ignite my imagination and stood safely on display.

Art was all around me, and had been from the start. Scattered everywhere throughout the house were African headrests and spindles and fabric and masks. Above the entrance door hung a black-bearded bug-eyed demon mask from Bali, which I was convinced would frighten off any would-be burglar. Tribal horns and spears and shields festooned the living room wall. I don't mean to overstate the case; our parents were not major collectors, but every time I climbed the stairs I climbed past Goya's *Tauromaquia,* a set of etchings rendering the stages of a bullfight. It was the air I breathed.

So it seemed only natural that, when I came to write things down, I wrote about visual art. Here is my final pronouncement:

> All artists are men—great men. Whether he is an unknown caveman, a Leonardo da Vinci, whether he is Toulouse-Lautrec or Albrecht Durer, if he is called Goya or Picasso he is still a man, united in the same purpose, that of putting what he thinks down on wood or paper. Only the way we imagine things and the way we put them down on canvas has changed through the centurys [*sic*]. Painting still is, and always will be, a noble business.
>
> THE END
>
> NICKY DELBANCO

Young Nicky would not today use the generalized term "men" for artists, and he would spell "centuries" correctly. Nor do I quite know what the author meant by "putting what he thinks down on wood." But the clarion call proclaimed by that eleven-year-old remains my credo still, and I'm struck by the through-line of his conviction that "painting . . . is a noble business . . ."

It was so, for my father, all his life. The juxtaposition of the two words —"noble" and "business"—seems telling to me now; he never could quite reconcile the two. As a businessman he was "artistic"; as a painter he was always hoping to earn profit from the work. This was a lifelong duality if not opposition, and it confused him from the start. Born in Hamburg, Germany, he was the second son of the director of an import-export firm; his father's father had been in the business too. The family was prosperous and well established. Although our surname, Delbanco, is Italian, my ancestors moved north from Venice in the mid-seventeenth century, having been bankers (aka moneylenders) there as long ago as 1570. They were the kind of upper-middle-class Jews who felt very much at home in and connected to society, and my paternal grandmother did have an eye for art. She collected such German Expressionists as Ernst Ludwig Kirchner and Emil Nolde and wore jewelry fashioned for her by Karl Schmidt-Rotluff. In her last years—she died more or less blind, in her mid-nineties—she herself would peeringly daub at a canvas, painting flowers there, or clouds.

Early on—Hamburg and Paris were the twin centers of such interest—the family acquired African totems and masks. At a time when European artists first paid attention to African art, my grandmother too fell under its spell; old photographs of the living room in Hamburg show tribal figures on tables and glowering down from pedestals. Although only a small portion of the things they owned survived the ravages of Hitler and the plundering zeal of the Nazis, theirs was a history of ownership as well as the desire to make something of and on their own.

My father was born in 1909 (he died ninety-eight years later) and from the very beginning had what his parents called—not, it seems, without raised eyebrows—"an artistic bent." He took drawing and art lessons in Hamburg; in America, once we'd moved here after a stint in London, he studied with Hans Hoffman and, later, Jack Levine. Towards the end of his life he made sculpture and went "abstract" in his compositions, trying to be part of what he called the zeitgeist and failing to break through. Although he won a prize or two and had several exhibitions, even a glowing notice in the *New York Times*, he never "made it" past a kind of affable amateur status.

Some of this, perhaps, had to do with the luck of the draw, some of it with his visible role as a collector and, in the end, art dealer. For several years he joined forces with and worked as an American representative of the eminent Swiss gallerist and collector Ernst Beyeler. This position put him in the purchaser and seller category as opposed to that of maker, and those who paid him visits did so more to look at the work of Piranesi or Monet than that of Delbanco. But mostly I think his lack of success arose from an error of judgment. He failed to honor his talent for drawing—preferring to work in an abstract and figure-ground mode for which he had no special gift. He produced hundreds of paintings, but it is the portraiture that counts.

As a portrait painter, he had impressive skill. Always, he kept a small notebook in his pocket, and at concerts or plays he would sketch the performer; in restaurants he would draw the waitress or waiter and offer their likeness as part of the tip. His studies of such figures as Max Eastman and Robert Moses incisively captured masked aspects of their character; his lifelong series of self-portraits unsparingly represent stages of age. His landscapes and still lifes were fluent, his eye for line and color keen. I loved my father, and though subjective judgment is involved here, I think it also the objective truth that he was a real artist who might have made a "go" of it except for the conflicting claims of being the head of a household: keeping food in the pantry and cars in the garage. My mother had no interest in conspicuous consumption, but she had high standards and was wont to say, "We are not rich enough to afford anything but the very best."

This meant, in effect, that my father worked much of his life in order to meet her exacting expectations. Raised in a mansion where nothing was denied her, she wished the same for her sons. The centuries-old tradition that the "head of the household" be the provider was one her husband never questioned, and he drove off every morning to work without complaint. If he felt trapped by the trappings of the bourgeoisie he never said so, and since our expenditures were large—three boys in private school, then college—his earnings had to keep pace. When he sold the Chagall or Courbet, it was to keep the household flush. Only towards the end did he wonder aloud, and then only musingly, what would have happened if he had chosen instead to follow the road not taken, and had tried to be an artist foremost and first.

In the way of such things, it was the expectation that the eldest son, my uncle Gustav, would take over the reins of the family business. But Gustav either had or feigned a nervous breakdown, saying he had no gift for or interest in commerce, and my grandparents relented. They gave him some art with which to bankroll his apprenticeship, and he made a sustained study of old master prints, then produced a PhD on the work of Abraham Bloemart, the Dutch painter and engraver (1566–1651). I like to imagine him in the Rijksmuseum or the Alte Pinakothek, calling up sheet after sheet of Rembrandt or Goltzius and learning what he chose to call their "handwriting." Soon enough, he put that knowledge to commercial use.

I will write of his gallery hereafter, and my time in it, but the present point is that my father was left holding the bag and effectively conscripted into his own father's line of work. He was allowed a *Wanderjahre* in which to paint and see the world, and would tell me stories of his sojourn in America—living in Greenwich Village and studying at the Art Students League. In New York, he attended Weill and Brecht's *Die Dreigroschenoper* in order to improve his English, once it had been presented here as *The Threepenny Opera*. Then he took a Greyhound bus cross-country and told me, unabashedly, that he failed to understand a proposition made to him, in Santa Fe, by a consort of the photographer Paul Strand, who suggested they might share a bed for the night.

How rapidly his innocence became experience is not for me to know, but in the early 1930s and his own mid-twenties he became a bristle merchant, returning to Hamburg to work in the import-export firm. For decades thereafter—first in England, then America, where he opened a branch of the family business—his focus was on international trade and the sale of such commodities as Chunking 2¾ bristles or Kolinsky sable brushes. His clients were painters and house-painters and those who manufactured industrial brushes and hair brushes and toothbrushes and brooms.

"Oh, what a falling-off was there," says Hamlet of his mother's decision to marry his uncle, once her beloved husband dies.

And though there's nothing tragic or Shakespearean in the story of my father's fate, it does seem to me a falling-off; he would have been far happier as an architect or artist. Instead he had been dutiful and followed his own father's lead.

The painter Max Liebermann (1847–1935) was a leading proponent of German Impressionism. He was born and died in Berlin, my mother's natal city. Of Ashkenazi descent, and wealthy, he produced more than two hundred commissioned portraits (of such notables as Albert Einstein and Paul von Hindenberg) as well as a series of self-portraits and portraits of his wife. He produced, in addition, many studies of landscape and horses and still lifes and street scenes—a man nearly always at work.

In 1920 he became the president of the Prussian Academy of Arts, resigning in 1933 when the academy decided no longer to exhibit the work of Jewish artists. He would have been forced to do so in any case under new restrictive laws, and when he died during the Third Reich his death went unacknowledged. Now, however, once again he's known as an authentic master—the German counterpart, though on a slightly smaller scale, of Édouard Manet.

In 1926, near the end of his lengthy career, he painted my maternal grandmother, Frances née Lehmann Bernstein. She sits in an armchair in what I assume was her own house, on Branitzer Platz—though possibly she went to Liebermann's residence, not the other way around. (There's a portrait of Liebermann's wife on a similar piece of furniture.) The background is indeterminate, a soft wash of color without identifying detail;

the only specific component of the portrait other than her person is the chair. Wood-rimmed and padded, with armrests, it's the sort of *fauteuil* that would have been fashionable at the time. Her dress too, a monochromatic brown, is fashionable if undistinguished. A white silk scarf lies knotted loosely at her throat.

Frances—I knew her as "Omi"—gazes straight ahead and slightly down. It's a sizable picture, life-size or a little larger, and though I remember her as petite and elderly, she's on the verge of monumental here. Her face dominates the portrait; her hands are crossed in her lap. Her knees are hidden by her brown dress; her legs drop down below the canvas's bottom edge.

In a more formal fashion, and with less inventiveness, the painting echoes Pablo Picasso's portrait of Gertrude Stein. Upright of posture, pensive—or, perhaps, merely patient—my grandmother stares at the painter, therefore viewer, her head on a slight tilt. The likeness antedates my personal knowledge of its subject by some twenty years, and time and the river had done their slow work on the unlined face here shown. Yet the face staring out and down at me is nonetheless familiar: an intelligent woman, *composed*.

The composition itself hung in the downstairs library of the house in Larchmont, New York—where, once we settled in America, my brothers and I were raised. It must have been a tutelary presence for Frances's daughter, my mother, reminding her of what was lost and what remained. Omi played the piano; she loved purple grapes and proper table manners and the poetry of Heinrich Heine; by the time I knew her—perhaps this had always been true—she did not join the conversation on politics or policy, the ways of the workaday world. (My paternal grandmother, Elsa—she of the penchant for African art—was different; she would complain that her capacious bed-and-sitting room in my uncle's house in London was less sizable than the Hamburg bathroom accorded to the upstairs maid.) In my hearing, at least, Frances never voiced regret for all that had been taken away and, from her large home, plundered; her disposition was complaisant and her manner gracious, kindly; and all of this I see in Liebermann's fine portrait of a woman absorbed in thought.

In my essay "A Visit to the Gallery," I considered what was lost:

> My maternal grandparents knew enough to leave Berlin for Paris as the Third Reich grew more threatful, though they left much behind. One of the things they took with them was a small oil painting by one of the six "founders" of Impressionism, Alfred Sisley. It's a beautiful canvas and a well-documented one—a boat hauled up on the shingle, in an open-air dry dock: *Bateaux en Reparation à St.-Mammes* (*Boats under Repair at St.-Mammes*). It has Sisley's signature water, beach, and sky; it's brilliantly composed and colorful—a kind of motion in stasis they carried with them, I suppose, as an emblem of what might be saved. When it came time to flee Paris, they entrusted the oil to a friend. A long and complicated history followed, with dealers' names like Cassirer and Durand-Ruel involved, with the thing hidden in an attic in the environs of Vichy and then somehow

sent to New York and Los Angeles, and just now fetching up for sale at Sotheby's in Manhattan.

I know about this because my grandfather did lodge a claim, as long ago as 1950, with the German government for reparation for confiscated art and household goods. There are organizations that help with the recovery effort and are superbly competent at research. I know, for example, the train my grandparents attempted to take out of Paris, the date they were turned back, and the date they succeeded in leaving; I know which camps they were interned in and when they were released. I know who attested to having seen the painting where, and the given names and middle names and surnames of those through whose hands it passed. I know who claimed to own it and what the claims consist of and how—via the Art Loss Register—they have been disproved. A cousin has a lawyer and the lawyer stopped the sale, and soon enough we'll know, perhaps, to whom the Sisley properly belongs . . .

There was much litigation, expenditure for legal work, and a settlement not properly germane to this discussion. But the question of inheritance does seem relevant, if only as an emblem of the presence of the past. That "black-bearded bug-eyed demon mask from Bali" now hangs in my own studio and, though I no longer believe it capable of warding off intruders, I write beneath its baleful glare with a sense of protected security: a talisman of time gone by that keeps me at the desk. My grandparents and parents are dead; *Bateaux en Reparation* has been sold, but in the storehouse of old memory I see the boats they—we—managed to travel on to this brave new world.

Now Frances hangs on my cousin Peter's wall and in the *catalogue raisonée* of Liebermann's life's work. It was not the "elder cousin" to whom I refer in my prefatory note on ART, but rather the son of my mother's brother, to whom she willed the painting. All this is of no consequence to anyone not directly involved, and soon or late there'll be none of us left, but the lady in the armchair is likely to endure. As my youthful self observed: "An interesting fact is that the word 'abstract' means 'to draw away from.'" Let us draw the curtain on her inward-facing gaze.

My father's elder brother, Gustav, had—by his own admission—"not a single artistic bone" in his body. But he was a scholar and a connoisseur and, in London as of the mid 1930s, a businessman who profited from the "import and export" of art. Along with two other equally knowledgeable partners—Henry Roland and Lillian Browse (the latter known as "The Duchess of Cork Street")—he founded an art gallery in a brick Queen Anne townhouse around the corner from the Burlington Arcade. Their specialty to start with was old masters, but they went so far into modernity as to represent Walter Sickert and Auguste Rodin. The first two floors of Roland, Browse & Delbanco were exhibition spaces; the basement was for storage and where they sat and chatted during mid-morning tea.

The top of the building contained more private rooms, where a favored client might look closely at a canvas and where the more important paintings and graphics were stored. All day long my uncle climbed or came down the steep flights of stairs, often carrying a work of art in one hand and a smoking pipe in the other.

He was small and lean and wiry, with a shock of snow-white hair. He had bright blue eyes and a pale, sharp-featured face—in his final years he powdered it pink—and paid no attention to social niceties. He would neglect to blow his dripping nose or forget appointments, but would remember, always, the location or the picture frame and subject of a Mantegna or Murillo he'd encountered years before.

One story, possibly apocryphal, reports on one of his clients, the king of Sweden. Of a given afternoon the king swept in with his entourage, and my uncle descended the stairs, then peered in his near-sighted way at the waiting visitor. "My good sir," Gustav said, "I perfectly remember your face, but I'm afraid I can't remember your name." The king proffered his hand and—an argument for royalty—responded, "Mr. Delbanco, I'm very glad to see you again. But I'm afraid I cannot remember your face!"

Absent-minded and inattentive, brusque, my uncle nonetheless had charm abounding and a puckish sense of humor. He liked good cheese and claret and the company of women and, after a trip to India, became a vegetarian. By gallery colleagues he was called "Professor" because of his pedantic manner and wide-ranging expertise in and knowledge of the history of art.

It was, I believe, the real thing. An early game I used to play with him went as follows: We would go to a museum or exhibition space together—and sometimes, to my certain knowledge, one he'd not entered before. Then I'd run up to an oil or object with its identifying label, and place my hand over the writing and ask him to tell me who was the particular artist or what the general provenance. The piece could be a fourteenth-century wood carving, a Chinese scroll, a Dutch landscape, a Renaissance devotional scene, or a portrait of a gentleman in furs. It could be Caravaggio, Cimabue, Correggio, or Cranach; it could be Klimt or Kokoshka. My uncle would stand a few feet distant, squinting, holding his unlit pipe, and after several seconds make his pronouncement: *X* or *Y* or *Z*.

He was never wrong. He always got it right. When I asked him how he knew or could identify the painter, he said, "Handwriting"; when I asked him how he knew the region from which an anonymous statue of the Virgin Mary derived and how he'd known, for example, that it was not from northern Germany, he said, "*Nein, nein, lower Rhine.*" Whether the caricaturist was Daumier, Forain, Gilray, or Hogarth he always knew which subject they reported on and which historical figure was satirized. Vague and forgetful about the diurnal world, the "absent-minded professor" proved accurate on art.

This was not the case for me. After having graduated from college, in 1963 I returned to London and went to work for Uncle Gustav and his partners in their gallery on Cork Street. By then the art trade was well established, and the establishment—catercorner to Bond Street and Saville Row—thrived. Lillian Browse was childless; Henry Roland's son had no interest in the profession of art dealer, and—again in the way of such things—it was clear though unstated that I would be heir apparent, if I learned and over time absorbed the procedures of the trade.

I was unsettled, a little, away from home and the girl I loved and, for the first time, living alone. My room was in a boarding house on Wetherby Gardens off Gloucester Road; there the bathroom was collective and the meter yielded, grudgingly, a shilling's worth of heat. I'd take the tube to work and serve as general dogsbody for the partners and the under-staff, running errands and carrying pictures and sitting at the entrance desk to greet those who walked in from the street. "Good morning, sir," I'd say or, "Good afternoon, madam," thinking this was common politeness—until I was told, in no uncertain terms, that it was indeed *common* politeness. The fellow who shined my shoes in the morning, or came by with tea, would say *sir* to me, but I shouldn't use the word with gallery patrons because it suggested an inferiority of social rank. Unless in fact they *were* a sir, in which case I was supposed to say, "Good morning, Sir William" or, "Good afternoon, Sir John . . ."

I learned when to address a lady by her given or her married name, and what the difference between "Lady Jane" or "Lady McMaster" entailed. I was told to keep a watchful eye on that threadbare, ill-shod fellow in the upstairs gallery because he was either a potential thief or, plausibly, an earl. I accompanied my uncle to auctions at Sotheby's or Christie's and went with him to frame makers and painting studios and on business trips to Scotland and, once, to visit the sculptor Henry Moore at home. The world of London's culture was expansive yet inter-connected; at my uncle's side I met *Sir* Kenneth Clark and Cyril Connolly, Iris Murdoch, Elias Canetti, and many other authors I was just starting to read. Aldous Huxley was a customer; so were J. B. Priestley and Cecil Day Lewis and the remnants of the Bloomsbury crew. It was a heady time.

Yet after a few months I found I could not be happy in London; its world was not my world. Although I had been born and, to a degree, raised in England, the social conventions of the place were no longer ones I felt easy with, or wanted to accept. One day my uncle took me aside and said, "This isn't working, is it? You're arriving at the gallery later and later each morning and you leave as soon as you can. Why don't we admit that this isn't for you; get out of here and write . . ."

This is the self-congratulatory version of the story, the one where our young hero espouses democratic principles and renounces the world of privilege and private dealing in favor of his own, and sullen, art. The other version—truer—is that I never knew enough about the field to make a go of it and wasn't willing to study. Week after month my uncle and I would walk into a room together; he'd know every painting there and I'd know that my feet were wet or that the girl in the corner wasn't wearing a brassiere or that in twenty minutes I might propose we have lunch. Sometimes, still, I think of it—the road not taken, the life unlived, and wonder what would have happened had my uncle and his partners been a little more interested in, as it were, the succession. I might have stayed in London or opened a dealership branch in New York. Then, instead of John Q. Public and an interested amateur I might have been professional and full of earned learned opinion and, like my uncle, a crank.

The last time he came to America he visited my family; he was in his nineties and, in short order, would die. As was the case with my father, a trip to see us in Ann Arbor always included a visit to the Detroit Institute of Arts and the museum in Toledo. Gustav had sold them both some paintings and liked to visit with, as he put it, his "old friends."

On the final day I took him to the University of Michigan's Museum of Art—which was displaying, with a certain amount of fanfare, a terra-cotta warrior and horse from the Han dynasty. These had arrived from Toronto and were being readied for an exhibition, which the sponsors claimed—with justification, since it was shortly after the discovery of these buried artifacts—would be the first showing of such treasures in the fifty states.

My uncle approached, was introduced, and asked if he might offer an opinion for the local press. I remember his response. "One of the advantages of great old age," he said, "is that we need not be respectful of the merely ancient. From an anthropological point of view, these objects have some value. But from an *artistic* standpoint, they are only rubbish." Then, leaning on his cane, he limped away to view a Max Beckman painting—*Begin the Beguin*—that he loved.

Back to that boy who, long years previous, knew the difference between Meindert Hobbema and his teacher, Jacob van Ruisdael. I ask myself now if elective affinity—a predisposition to a subject—is instinctual or earned. Who knows why *A* can sit at a piano and, with no instruction, pick out a tune, whereas *B* takes years of music lessons and remains thick-fingered and tone-deaf? Who knows why *C* remembers poetry with no seeming effort and *D,* no matter how serious and scrupulous, forgets? At every dinner table there's someone who can offer up the middle name of a senator from Iowa and someone else who can't recall if a politician comes from Indiana or Illinois. We have, each one of us, a skill set slightly different from our neighbor's, and there's not much point in trying to discover the source of the distinction: It's an apple or an orange, born or bred.

Now when I re-read our eleven-year-old Nicky, I'm reminded of his love of unearned generality: "Painters began also not only to paint pictures of religious meaning but to make landscapes and human figures. Of course the church tried to rule this down but near the beginning of the 1500's there were more and more pictures of things around us. This showed a minute pulling away from the stiffness of the church and helped to free men's minds even more. A very definite trend towards a new life had started!"

Or: "As I have tried to stress in this book, the styles of different countries could change very quickly. Therefore the realism of the great Dutch masters and the rigidness of the French could be found in many a different country than that of the originator of the style."

I won't quote him further. Young Nicky did possess impressive information, but his text is chockablock with pronouncements of this sort: a pedant in the making with a penchant for the overview, a boy who bit off rather more than he could plausibly chew. *RIP.*

In those early years, I tried my hand at painting. At my parents' suggestion I took an art class in Larchmont and was instructed by a local teacher how to prepare a canvas or mix paints on a palette. We painted, assiduously, apples and vases and houses and trees; we sketched our teacher's daughter as she sat in the room with a book. When I brought back a finished canvas for my father's scrutiny, he squinted, examined it closely, and smilingly shook his head. Then he patted me on mine. On weekends I would paint by his side, in his third-floor studio, using a small wooden easel propped up beside his own. Or we would set up outdoor easels on the shore of the Long Island Sound, drawing sailboats and boulders and ducks. I filled sketch pads with studies of horses and cowboys, and houses with chimneys and windows and doors.

The doors stayed shut. The windows gave on nothing and the chimneys had no smoke. At a given moment—some years after my disquisition on ART—I recognized I had no gift for it, at least in the visual mode. My painted river resembled blue pavement; my pine tree looked much like an oak. My portraits were inadvertent caricatures, and the faces—male or female, young or elderly—all seemed cut from the same cloth. It took me longer than it should have to understand that what powered my book were not the paintings reproduced but the language I used to describe them; here lay my true interest as well as, possibly, my gift.

For better or for worse, this perception has remained with me through the ensuing years. Each morning when I sit to write I feel that ancient hunter's reverent elation when he drew an image on the rock-wall of a cave. "Perhaps the caveman threw stones at his masterpiece." Then he might emerge to track actual quarry and, every once in a great while, succeed.

What follows are three memories of three major authors who influenced me greatly, each in different ways. I'm aware that my models all are male—less surprising, perhaps, in the period of which I write than would be the case today. And there have been many women who became close colleagues, from whose instruction and friendship I profited in the world of words. But it's the flat fact of my education that the three writers and teachers I here memorialize are men.

The first—John Updike—taught me what a leader-disciple relation entails, the second—John Gardner—taught me about colleagueship, the third—James Baldwin—exemplified what open-handed generosity might mean. If I had to reduce their instruction to a single statement, I learned from the first about an intensity of attention to language, from the second about unswerving devotion to craft. From the third I learned that prose, no matter how carefully composed or revised, must stand in the service of faith: the faith that words, in times of trouble, count. Their lessons have remained with me; throughout my years as teacher they were ones I tried hard to impart. It shocks me now to know that—in chronological terms—I've become the senior author of this company; in memory, they stay my elders still.

I have been the full-fledged student of a writer only once. John Updike was one of the most literate and able critics of our time. His breadth of reading, acuity of insight, and grace of expression must give most scholars pause; he would no doubt have been made welcome at any institution in any of the fifty states. But he

My mother around the age of twenty in Berlin

My maternal grandparents' house on Branitzer Platz in Berlin, showing a wing that was bombed during World War II but later rebuilt

The living room of my father's house in Hamburg, with German expressionist art on the walls and African art on the tables

My grandparents, Ludwig and Elsa Delbanco, in their garden on the Outer Alster in Hamburg, circa 1933

Nicholas standing across the Grand Canal from the Venetian palazzo occupied by ancestors in the sixteenth century. Photo by Elena Delbanco.

The house on Concord Road in Ann Arbor, Michigan, where we lived for thirty years

Our rented home, "la petite maison,"
in Chateauneuf de Grasse, France

My parents, Barbara and Kurt Delbanco,
playing chess in London, circa 1944

A family portrait on the stoop in our Larchmont, New York, house. *Rear row*: my brother Thomas and our parents; *front row*: Nicholas, our dog Mr. Chips, and my brother Andrew.

Our wedding day in Pawlet, Vermont, 1970

Elena with Francesca as an infant, in Wellfleet, 1974. Photo by Tomas Breuer.

With Andrea in rehearsal for my play, *Wolf,* in Ann Arbor, 1988

Andrea and Francesca, Lake George, 1981

With Major Scobie,
in Ann Arbor, 1984.
Photo by Joseph McCune.

Nicholas and Elena (in her wedding dress) at a "Victorian Ball" in Vermont, 1979

Sitting in "Churchill's Chair." The Churchill War Rooms, London, 2023. Photo by Nicholas Stoller.

remained at a stiff arm's remove from academe, earning his living by the pen alone. In the summer of 1962, however, his resolution wavered and he agreed to teach—at Harvard Summer School. I wanted to remain in Cambridge and applied for the course. It was an offhand decision; I had only read a little of his work. When he accepted me into his fiction workshop, it would have been ungrateful to drop out.

In retrospect, I see more clearly how lucky and right was that choice. The first word I wrote for Updike was the first of my first novel. Like any self-respecting undergraduate, I intended to be either a poet, folk singer, or movie star. I considered "prose" and "prosaic" to be cognate terms. (They are, admittedly, but I know something more by now about the other three professions and would not trade.) The young man's fancy is poetic, and his models are Rimbaud or Keats. Mine were, at any rate; my first compositions were suicide notes. But I was signed up for a writing workshop with no idea of what to write and not much time to decide. The day of that decision is vivid to me still.

A friend and I were strolling around a lake in Wellesley; we'd been reading for final exams. I heard him out as to his future; then he had to listen to me. I had tried my hand already at the shorter stuff, I said; I was going to write a novel. That was what a summer should consist of—something ambitious, no piddling little enterprise like Chekhov's but something on the scale of, let's say, *Moby Dick*.

Yet before I wrote my masterpiece I had to plan it out. What do first novels consist of, I asked—then answered, nodding sagely at a red-haired girl in a bikini emerging from the lake. First novels by men are either the myth of Narcissus or the parable of the Prodigal Son—but generally inadvertent. Their authors do not understand that they fit an ancient mold. I already knew enough about Narcissus, I confessed, and therefore would elect the latter; I'd rewrite the parable. The difference was that my revision would be conscious, whereas most young novelists fail to see themselves in sufficiently explicit mythic terms.

That was not my problem, but there *were* problems to solve. I knew nothing about the landscape of the Bible (in Luke 15:11–32), and needed to find a substitute. My friend lit a cigarette; we considered. It happened that I'd been to Greece the previous summer and traveled wide-eyed for weeks. I would replace one location with the other. The Prodigal Son has three component parts: The son leaves home, spends time away, and returns. My novel too would have three components, with Rhodes and Athens as its locales. My Greek protagonist would go from the island to the city and, as in the parable, "eat up his substance with whores."

The girl in the bikini trailed drops of water where she walked; she shook her long hair free. She rounded a bend in the path. I instructed my friend that *hetarae* in Athens had "Follow Me" incised backwards on their sandals, so that they could print directions in the dust. The question of contemporaneity engaged me for three minutes. I knew enough about modern-day Greece to fake it, possibly, but knew I'd never know enough about the ways of antique Attica; the sign on the prostitute's sandal exhausted my store of lore. It would take less research to update the parable. And there, within ten minutes, I had it: a contemporary version of the story of the Prodigal Son that followed the text faithfully and yet took place in Greece. The rest was an issue of filling in blanks; I started to, next week.

I have told this tongue-in-cheek, but it is nonetheless true. The epigraph of *The Martlet's Tale* is the first line of the parable; the great original is buried in my version, phrase by phrase. I revised the novel many times and by the time I'd finished was no longer a beginner.

However, looking back I'm astonished; it all fell so neatly in place. An editor at J. B. Lippincott ushered me into his office and agreed to bring out the book. "You're a very fortunate young man," he said, but I thought his politeness routine. I took success for granted when it came. My photograph in magazines seemed merely an occasion for judging the likeness; a long and flattering review in the *New York Times* on publication day was no more than an author expected; I ate expensive lunches with the cheerful certainty that someone else would pay.

In some degree, this very blindness worked to my advantage. I had been accustomed to a schoolboy's notion of success and would have dealt with failure far less equably. Had Updike not encouraged me, I cannot say for certain if I would have persevered; there were many wind-scraps in the wind, and I followed the favoring breeze. Harvard does prepare you for the world in this one crucial way: If you succeed within its walls, you assume that you will when outside. When I handed in the first chapter of *The Martlet's Tale* and my teacher's reaction was praise, I concluded that the rest must follow as the night does day. I suppose I stood out in his class; I certainly tried to; his wary approval meant much. I wrote a second chapter and was hooked.

The hook went deep. Through later years and decades, Updike remained my model. His was the opinion I most valued, the endorsement I most sought. We saw each other frequently to start with, less frequently as time went on and I moved away from Vermont. The last encounter was by happy accident, at an exhibition in Manhattan that we both were walking through. I'd lunched with John not long before, at a prearranged meeting in Boston, but this felt somehow more important because unscheduled: the chance to look at art with him and see, from a shared vantage, what he saw.

As always he instructed me: the context he established, the minutiae he observed, the things he was aware of that I failed to register. Each time we paused to focus (on photographs of post-Katrina New Orleans, in the Metropolitan Museum of Art) he pointed out something I might not have noticed, or surely not so rapidly and surely not so well. *Just Looking* and *Still Looking,* his collections of art criticism, attest to his alertness and wide-ranging eye.

Once I drove him on a road near Bennington I'd driven over often—past a house I passed on an almost daily basis but that my passenger had never seen before. John made a remark about the "shuddering roof line" of the ancient structure, and then the way the shutters were hung, and I realized to my respectful shame that he in one assessing glance had captured what in hundreds of trips I had failed to see. Henry James's injunction—"Try to be someone on whom nothing is lost"—fit Updike perfectly; nothing escaped his attention.

My relation to him, always, was that of admiring acolyte—and though in later years I did muster reservations and oppositional opinions, he was my teacher, first and last. He was, I think, not sorry to claim me as his student, and I was always proud to claim that as my role. There were letters exchanged, books signed and sent, postcards and photographs shared. His archive at Harvard's Houghton Library is vast, and I play only a modest part in it, but one of his last letters to me is a text I cherish and reprinted in *Lastingness: The Art of Old Age.* In it Updike resoundingly writes: "Aesthetic flourishes fade and wrinkle, though they may get attention when new. A blunt sincerity outlasts finely honed irony, I would think."

His work was full of "aesthetic flourishes" and "finely honed irony"; in the end there was "a blunt sincerity" as well.

The cover illustration of one of John Gardner's collections of short stories, *The Art of Living,* shows a motorcyclist racing at the reader, straight ahead. His jacket is black leather, as was John's, and his expression is grim. It is as though he drives *In the Suicide Mountains*—another of the author's titles—prepared to take the leap described on the final page of *Grendel*; there are fierce night rides throughout his work, and creatures everywhere at risk.

John Champlain Gardner Jr. died of injuries sustained in a motorcycle accident on Tuesday, September 14, 1982. The afternoon was balmy, bright; the roads were dry. He was an experienced driver, a few miles from home; he swerved—to avoid another vehicle, perhaps?—and fell. John was forever trying to explain himself, but death is inexplicable; the coroner's report describes result, not cause. It's clear he was trying to make it, fighting to survive. We never will know what he saw while he fell, or felt when the handlebar dealt him its mortal gut punch.

He maintained, repeatedly, he had no fear of death; he wanted the rider of *The Art of Living* to appear playful, not fierce. On September 16, two days after the accident, Elena and I received a letter from him full of future plans. He was to marry a third time on the weekend of what became his funeral; he was immersed in a translation of *Gilgamesh*: "Fine pome!" He sounded, as always, vividly alive.

John seemed somehow to have been born with a quicker ratio to the passage of time than the rest of us. He worked with a headlong, hurtling rush—at times, twenty hours a day. Each new home for him, I think, was absolutely home; each new set of friends was dear and old and gifted; his moderation was our excess and his excess brooked no containment. It's not so much a question of the forced march and furious pace, as if he knew he might die young and wanted to waste or miss nothing. Rather, it was as if he decided that artistic matters demanded all the patient seriousness he had. There was no attention left to squander on sleep or table manners or the IRS . . .

Others knew him longer and more intimately. I offer this account of friendship in the knowledge that it was representative; many shared in the general loss. We met on Tuesday, April 16, 1974. I was teaching at Bennington College, and he was on a reading tour; he and his wife, Joan, arrived for dinner at our house on Spraguetown Road.

My first impression of Gardner remains: a rotund, pipe-smoking man, with a high-pitched voice and rapid rate of utterance, pontificating splendidly and as if by rote. His eyes were red-rimmed, his white hair lank; he made his entry two hours late. It was not his fault, in fact; it was Albany Airport's, and the fog's. But somehow, in the ensuing years, there would always be some such disruption: A car would fail to start or end up in a ditch, a snowstorm would come out of nowhere, a wallet would be misplaced. Joan Gardner wore expensive clothing and fistfuls of jewelry; the novelist wore blue jeans and a cracked black leather vest. He emptied a near-full quart of vodka before we sat to eat.

I saw him often in such situations later; they are hard to avoid. Fame brings a constant, admiring assault, a request from civil strangers to be brilliant or outrageous or at least informed. It wears one down and forces one to substitute mask for face; sooner or later, they fuse. This is doubly a danger for the writer, since privacy is the sine qua non of his work and he has had no training in the actor's life.

By midnight I had dropped my guard; by two o'clock he had too. Elena—eight months pregnant—went to sleep. Since I had to teach the next morning, I tried to call a halt; I had to prepare for my class.

Nonsense, said John, we'd have another bottle and he'd help me through the morning session—what was it on, by the way? "Virginia Woolf," I said, and construed his nodding to mean knowledge of her work. We talked till four or five and met again at ten o'clock; I weaved my way to class.

In the event I did most of the teaching. Perhaps I knew more about Virginia Woolf; certainly I felt more responsible to the students than did their visitor. I lectured with a panicky inventiveness, stopping only for questions or breath. The session went well; I knew that. But Gardner assured me, with what I later came to recognize as characteristic hyperbole, that it was the best talk he'd ever attended—at least, on any author after Malory. He knew something more than I did, maybe, about Apollonius of Rhodes. I was gratified, of course, and all the more so when his wife said he repeated the praise to her later; we had become "fast friends." The next night, after his reading, I asked if he wanted a job.

I was in the position to hire him but did not believe he'd accept. It was more an offhand courtesy, a variety of "If you'd ever care to come back through . . ." To my surprise he said yes. He was tired of his present appointment, possibly; his family hoped to move east. At the end of *Stillness*—a posthumously published autobiographical novel, for which I served as editor—he records the accidental-seeming sequence that brought him to Vermont. We were in his motel room; he was changing shirts. This completes my introductory image: a white-fleshed, big-bellied man with pants rolled up, his pipe smoking on the coverlet, and papers all over the bed.

Students clustered at the motel entrance, waiting to whisk him away. The last thing that he handed me was a drawing of himself as gnome, peeping out from bushes with the block-letter legend, "Should Nicholas require John Gardner, he can be reached at . . ." (his number and address in Illinois). I did require him, and he could be reached.

For three years thereafter, we saw each other continually. His presence was a gift. He ballyhooed my work in public and berated it in private. Day in, week out, we wrangled over prose. There was nothing polite or distanced about his sense of colleagueship; if he hated a line he said so, and if he hated a character he said so all the more loudly. At this remove it's hard to remember what we discussed at such length: profluence, *energeia,* walnut trees. I spent three days hunting through graveyards and telephone books to prove that Sherbrooke with a terminal *e*—the surname of a character in the novel I was writing—would be more likely than Sherbrook without. He came up with a whiskey bottle spelled Sherbrook; I pointed to a Sherbrooke township south of Montreal. We cotaught classes and founded a summer writing workshop together. Out of many memories I will here cite two.

October Light was accorded the National Book Critics Circle Award for fiction in 1976. The presentation ceremony took place in New York, and John's publishers made it an occasion. They hosted a supper party afterwards, and a suite was reserved in Gardner's name at the Algonquin Hotel. He asked Elena and me to be his companions that night. He wore the dungarees we'd seen him wear all month; the two of us dressed to the nines. He was energetic, affable—but most of all, and in a way that's impossible to overstate, he was serious. Where other writers would have rested on their laurels, he was busy lobbying for his present project—an opera. He was no good at small talk, too abrupt; he was busy all night long.

This helps explain his torrential outpouring those years; he did not stop. His first question to me, always, was, "What are you working on?" *October Light* was finished, therefore irrelevant.

The occasion was a success. There were important and beautiful people, good speeches and fine wines. At night's end we repaired to the Algonquin, where they nearly refused him a bed. He had a portable typewriter and briefcase as luggage, no credit cards or cash. We somehow convinced the desk clerk that Alfred Knopf himself would foot the bill, and were escorted to the suite. There were flowers and fruit, bottles waiting on ice; we ordered brandy as well. As the bellhop left, John sat. The couch was vast. He sank in its plush lushness, and mice scrambled from his feet.

They were gone quickly; they scurried to some other section of the suite. But in that first instant I thought they emerged from his boots. We laughed. We placated Elena and informed the bellhop on his return that he should make certain hereafter to clear away the cheese. Yet the image remains and retains its first power to shock: I saw his power in the process of collapse.

The telephone rang. At home he would answer, "Hello, Gardners." That was, he explained, a way of being noncommittal; it was a large family, and you never knew which person the caller intended. It was also a way of keeping celebrity seekers at bay; you didn't have to say, "John Gardner" and could therefore always say he wasn't in.

It rang again. He answered, "Hello, Gardner." He seemed forlorn; the brandy and Book Critics Circle Award had no power to invigorate. He was white and tired and, for all our efforts at support, alone.

Within the year, he was operated on for cancer. His first marriage had ended; his second—to a Bennington graduate, the poet L. M. Rosenberg—was in the offing, and he had moved from Vermont. They took him to Johns Hopkins Medical Center for emergency surgery; on Christmas I flew down. At dawn on

Christmas Day the airports are deserted, so I had an empty, easy flight and arrived in Baltimore by nine.

He had not expected me and was watching television. His usual pallor was more pronounced still and made the sheet seem colorful. When he saw me, he blushed. It was, I teased him, the first and only time he'd been caught in the act of watching TV; James Page, the protagonist of John's *October Light,* had shot out the television screen in his house. So it would not have been pleasure but embarrassment that caused him to flush—but it was all right, I assured him; his secret addiction was safe. I blathered on like that until we felt at ease with silence; against hospital rules he lit up his pipe; all was well. I presented Christmas tokens; he complained about the trouble he was having with a paragraph; he had worked at it for three days now, but it wasn't right. The medicine tray held his IBM Selectric Typewriter, and the window ledge was heaped with twenty-weight bond. (The next time I visited him at Hopkins he was sitting up in bed and busily at work—irritable, almost, at the interruption. The third time Elena came too, and we could not find him; he was in the reaches of the hospital basement, having commandeered a Xerox machine. But that first instant when I watched him through the open door remains the image here.) I knew—to see him reaching for the TV monitor and then for his pipe, turning even this cell into a work space, disorderly—he would survive.

His work will. Novelist, poet, critic, playwright, librettist, scholar, translator, fabulist: At forty-nine years old, he had the exuberance and protean energy of men not half his age. He was involved in the theater, music, woodworking, publishing, teaching, painting—any number of pursuits and none of them casual or slapdash. His paintings were intensely seen; his boxes and furniture served. I remember dropping by his house in Bennington to find so many bookshelves fabricated in one day that I thought the pipe smoke he stood wreathed in had caused my eyes to blur.

He did seem, somehow, multiple. The first musical selection of the memorial service on East Main Street in Batavia—the town in upstate New York where he was born and buried—was a cassette of John and his son, Joel, performing on their French horns. They played "Amazing Grace."

More than half my life ago, I was a near neighbor of James Baldwin. We'd met in the winter of 1970, briefly, in Istanbul. I was working on the screenplay for the film of my first novel, and the director knew Baldwin, and Baldwin was in town. We had a drink together and went to *Fortune and Men's Eyes*, a play he directed in Turkish. Not knowing Turkish, I was less than enthralled, and the meeting did not matter much and the evening was a blur. The following year, Elena and I moved to the south of France as newlyweds, and we ran into Baldwin in Cannes. Standing on line at the American Express office, in what seemed like an interminable forward progress, I recognized the writer behind me. We shook hands. Then I said that the director who had introduced us would be passing through, and maybe we could get together for a meal or drink.

I was surprised by his alacrity; we went to his house the next day. Elena's daybook for our final ten days in Provence lists five such occasions: dinner at his house, at ours, at a restaurant in Saint-Paul-de-Vence, talks and walks. He was completing *No Name in the Street*; he was planning to remain in France and would do so for years. His openhanded welcome, his insistence that we call as soon as we came back meant much, as did his cheerful certainty that we would return.

In 1973, when we settled again in the house in Provence, Baldwin treated us like long-lost friends. He had established a work pattern and an entourage. He had a chauffeur large enough to double as a bodyguard, a cook, a companion named Philippe who acted as a kind of secretary-manager, and various others whose function is less easy to describe. There would be a dancer or painter in tow—old lovers or associates from some project in the offing, or projected, or long past. They came from Italy, America, Algeria, Tunisia, Finland. Brothers and nephews passed through.

We were rarely less than six at table, and more often ten. The cook and the *femme de ménage* came and went; the men stayed on. They treated their provider with a fond deference, as if his talent must be sheltered from invasive detail, the rude importunate matters of fact. They answered the phone and the door. They sorted mail. There was an intricate hierarchy of rank, a jockeying for position that evoked nothing so much as a Provencal court—who was in favor, who out, who had known Jimmy longer or better or where, who would do the shopping or join him in Paris for the television interview or help with the book-jacket photo. He was working, again, on a novel: *If Beale Street Could Talk.*

Baldwin drank scotch. We drank wine. I have not as yet described the quality of kindness in his manner, the affection he expected and expressed. His face is widely known—that dark glare, broad nose, those large protruding eyes, the close-fitting cap of curls then starting to go white. But photographs cannot convey the mobile play of feature, the intensity of utterance, the sense he could contrive to give that attention *matters* and gesture can count. There was something theatrical in Jimmy's manner, and it grew automatic at times. He would embark on what seemed a tirade, a high-speed compilation of phrases that clearly had been phrased before, a kind of improvised lecture spun out of previous speech. He stared at you unblinkingly; you could not turn away. He wore expensive jewelry and fingered it, talking; he smoked. He had been holding center stage for years.

You shifted in your seat. You said, "Yes, but..." and he raised his imperious manicured hand. Dialogue, for Baldwin, was an interrupted monologue; he would yield the platform neither willingly nor long. He could speak incisively on a book he had not read. But again and again he impressed me with his canny ranging, his alert intelligence. In the literal sense, I was no longer a student, but Baldwin remained a teacher at least as much as (from his own early training) a preacher.

"Understand me," he would say. "It's important you understand." And it *was* important, and in that mesmeric presence you thought you understood...

My pleasure in our meetings is easily explained. Here was the spokesman of his generation and color speaking directly to me. That he took my opinions seriously, that he read and respected my work, or appeared to, that he wanted us with him as often as possible—all this was flattering. When we parted late at night, Jimmy would say, "See you two tomorrow." If we came for lunch instead, he urged us to stay on for dinner; when a friend passed through Saint-Paul, he would insist we meet.

Why he wanted to spend time with us is less clear. Each friendship partakes of the reciprocal trade agreement, and I can only speculate as to Baldwin's motives in the trade. He was the most sociable of solitaries; though constantly attended and attended to, he held himself apart. He wanted to hear "news from home." Elena had worked several years in a rehabilitation agency for drug addicts in New York, whose clientele was largely black; she moved easily through his old streets.

Though almost without exception the single woman in his house—and in a party of a dozen men—she was given pride of place. She sat at his right hand. They liked each other, I believe, with unfettered immediate liking; she treated him with just the right mixture of impatience and respect. They embraced each other, meaning it; they huddled in corners together. There was nothing exclusionary about his attitude to women; though surrounded by adoring boys, he was also a "family man."

I mattered to him, I suppose, as a practitioner of a shared trade. He told me he was starved for the chance to talk books, for a discussion, say, of Henry James with someone who had read him. We talked the way most writers do, in a kind of shorthand and sign language. We asked each other, always, how the work had gone that day, how this paragraph was progressing, or that character and scene . . .

Jimmy's acolytes believed the process sacramental, as if behind his study door strange rituals took place. He would shut himself away at midnight and somehow produce an object to which accrued money and fame. They had little sense, it seemed, of how much it was costing him to keep them all in style, or the anxious private wrangling in the watches of the night. His acclaim had diminished of late, and he knew I knew it. The alchemy of which his friends were confident was less mysterious to me and therefore more compelling; he worked at continual risk. And I was moved by his intensity, his struggle with a form that had come to seem elusive. *Beale Street* is not as finely honed as *Go Tell It on the Mountain* or *Giovanni's Room.* That Baldwin had been consequential to a multitude of readers made all of this more poignant; he had made himself the benchmark to be passed.

Much of what I knew of the plight of the black American I had learned from reading him. And what sometimes seemed like paranoia could be argued as flat fact. The assassination of Malcolm X, Medgar Evers, Martin Luther King, Bobby Kennedy, George Jackson, the named and nameless legion of the near and distant dead, his own impending fiftieth birthday, the sickness of a beloved friend and mentor, the painter Beauford Delaney—all weighed heavily that winter.

"This face," he'd say, and frame it with his slender glinting fingers. "Look at this crazy face."

In the early 1970s Richard Nixon reigned unchallenged. The Watergate scandal was building but the hearings had not yet begun. Each day brought more darkness to light. We rushed out for the paper and listened to the radio daily, but a "smoking gun" or upheaval in the political affairs of France could trigger no equivalent concern. One sign of national allegiance is the reaction to political scandal: We waited like literal exiles for the summons to return. The French took presidential corruption for granted, but we were transfixed. Although it curdled into scorn, we discussed America with the fervor of the unrequited lover. We went for walks or dawdled over drinks; we visited each other ("Hey, baby, what's up?" "Hey, darlin', where've you *been*?") often and often those months.

Elena and I had been at his house in Saint-Paul-De-Vence two or three times in a row; it was our turn to invite the Baldwin clan. We did so, one Thursday, for lunch. They said they would come, happily; they were seven, maybe nine. The two members of his party I remember as men passing through were a dancer called Bernard and a publisher named Willi. The former was lean, lithe, beautiful, and black; he had danced at the Folies Bergère. The latter was mountainous, white. We had been warned about his appetite by Baldwin's cook days before; Willi was a voracious eater who had sent her to the market three times that afternoon.

Elena planned a *navarin*; we made an extra pot. A *navarin*, though simple, takes time to prepare; we started the previous day. We peeled turnips and carrots and leeks. We cubed the lamb and browned it, then fashioned the *bouquet garni*. Our landlady knocked. She was hoping we might join her tomorrow for lunch; there were people she thought we should meet.

Lilo Rosenthal was eighty years old; she owned the property of which we occupied the gatehouse, and she was being generous to her youthful tenants. But we made our excuses, inviting her in; as she could see we too were preparing a meal. We would be unable to join or invite her, for we owed a friend a thank-you *navarin.* I remember not naming his name. Part of this was inverse snobbery, a distaste for glitter by association, and partly the suspicion that, had Lilo known Baldwin was coming, we should have had to invite her. They would have been water and oil.

At any rate, she told us, she hoped we would take in our wash. It hung on the clothesline outside. She intended to walk by *la petite maison* and let her friends take photographs; they were passionate photographers. Her friends were distinguished, she said. They were the last of the Hapsburgs and the last of the Hohenzollerns, respectively. Or perhaps they were the last of the Schleswigs and Holsteins, or collateral branches instead. In any case they were old and distinguished and would not appreciate the laundry on our line. She hoped we would ready the house.

We promised. We made the second *navarin,* brought an extra half-dozen bottles from the *cave,* bought three additional *boules* from the baker, and waited for Jimmy to come. He himself did not drive. He had, however, purchased a brand new Mercedes, dark brown and substantial, just short of stretch limousine size. His driver would be working that day, he had assured me, and he was bringing Bertrand, Daro, Philippe, Billy, Willi, and Bernard.

At the appointed hour we were ready; a car came. The day was overcast. What pulled into the parking space between our gatehouse and the villa was not Jimmy's Mercedes but an ancient gray Renault. It was followed, funereally, by a Deux Chevaux. Lilo Rosenthal appeared. Her guests emerged. They were slow and small and bent. The process of arrival took some time. The doors opened, faltered, closed. The last of the Hapsburgs and the last of the Hohenzollerns wore dark suits and carried cameras and advanced with umbrellas and canes. They shuffled off together to their hostess's house.

As soon as they were out of sight we heard another car. The deep-throated growl of gears, the high hum of power in harness, the trumpeting bravura of the horn—and Baldwin's Mercedes roared up. It spat the raked gravel; it rocked on its brakes; it fairly pirouetted in the sudden sun. Four doors flung wide in unison; our company had come!

They were dressed for the occasion, grandly. They wore boaters and foulards. Their boots gleamed. Bernard especially was splendid; he emerged twirling his scarf and waist-sash of pink silk. He did a few dance steps and flung his hat high and extended his hands for applause. We applauded. Jimmy embraced us; we, him. The chauffer was not happy with the switchbacks of the entry drive. "They're badly banked," he said. He had brought his lunch along and elected to stay with the car. He stood, arms folded, glowering down through the olive groves; he was Danish, thick and stolid and impervious to charm.

"What a charming place," the publisher proclaimed. We piloted them in.

This was not easy; they swarmed. They raced to the crest of the meadow and walked tiptoe along the rim of the irrigating cistern that doubled as a pool. They approved the view. They clattered through our little house, exclaiming at the style of it, posing on the bedroom balcony. "Give me the simple life," they chorused. "Let's have *la vie en rose*." Philippe had brought flowers; he garlanded Elena, Daro, Jimmy, Willi, and Bernard. We emptied four bottles of wine by the time we settled to eat.

The *navarin* was a success. The publisher, Willi, approved. Audibly, he sighed, sitting back on the banquette and rolling up his sleeves. "Which pot's for me?" he asked. There were olives and pâté. There was much laughter, celebration, conversation, praise for the salads and bread. The dining room could barely contain us; we rolled about the table like a litter of puppies, suckling, jostling, slicing sausages and cheese and fruit and cake. A shadow appeared at the window. I looked up.

Lilo Rosenthal was outside by the car. She and her four companions were inching up to the house. They had their cameras at shoulder level, focusing, and it pained them, clearly, to approach.

We must have looked, to them, like Spengler's nightmare realized: the decline of the West. The beaming black man at the center, the lithe array around him, the voluminous white man with loaves in his hands, the young hosts plying everyone with wine, the pyramid of bottles, the ruckus of festivity, the Mercedes being polished—all this was hard to focus on or frame. I could see Lilo explaining. I do not know how she explained.

There was no laundry, however. They circled warily. We did not invite them in. They moved to the back of the house.

America selects, each year, a few apprentice artists to celebrate and spotlight. In 1966, when *The Martlet's Tale* was published, I was one of those fortunate few. A laudatory review came out on publication day in the *New York Times Sunday Book Review* and, soon thereafter, in the pages of the daily *Times*. An eminent Greco-American author, in the *Saturday Review*, said he wished he could have written as good a book at twenty-three, but knew he could not have done so. I met him many years later, and he called me Nikos, assuming I must be Greek. My picture was in magazines and displayed in the window of bookstores; the English edition called the book, as though there were others, "Delbanco's Novel" and, almost as an afterthought, printed the title too.

Soon enough I signed a contract for a film, which was produced in Rome. Together with the director, I was to write the screenplay. (Somewhere in my archive, and occupying pride of place, is a full-page ad in *Variety*, announcing that in Dinecitta they were shooting Federico Fellini's *The Clowns*, Luchino Visconti's *Death in Venice*, and Nicholas Delbanco's *The Martlet's Tale*.)

To have been part of that trio was to have arrived, though I would have preferred the listing in alphabetical and not—after Fellini and Visconti—to be the third of three. Neither I nor the director was as yet thirty years old, and *Variety* made much of us, extolling the spirit of youth. It was the time of *Easy Rider* and the widespread warning to trust no one over thirty; in all seriousness I was asked to add some scenes of my hero riding motorcycles down an empty beach...

In 1969, while the film was being green-lit, I met with the producers in New York. There were, among others, the executive producer, the story editor, the director, and me; we gathered in the town house on Park Avenue where the principal financier lived. This was the period when Greece was under the thumb of a military junta (1967–1974) and its leader, Colonel Georgios

Papadopoulos. In my youthful fervor I put a condition on the making of *The Martlet's Tale* as a movie: that it not be shot in Greece.

I did not want, I said at the meeting, to give any further countenance or money to a country ruled by fascists. I was honored at the prospect of a treatment based on what I wrote but would not permit the location and establishing shots to take place in the novel's locale. It was a deal-breaker: yes or no.

"All right, kid," said the producer, Tweedle-Dee.

"OK," said the executive producer, Tweedle-Dum.

"We hear you," said the story editor, whom I will call Tweedle-X.

They looked at each other a minute. "It's no big thing, the islands," said Tweedle-Dee.

"We can do an island someplace else," agreed Tweedle-X.

"Yeah, Italy," said the money man.

"Sicily, maybe," said Tweedle X.

Tweedle Dum agreed. "It's got sand, it's got donkeys and olive trees and marble. It's got temple ruins."

"Right, Agricento. Better than Greece, if you ask me," said Tweedle-Dee. He lit a cigar.

"But what about the Acropolis, kid?" asked Tweedle-Dum. "How do we do the Acropolis in the city part of the story? You've got scenes on the Acropolis, am I right or am I right?"

My book—in accordance with the parable of the Prodigal Son—had three parts. The hero lives on the island of Rhodes, leaves it and goes to the big city, then returns to the island and his true forsaken love. And since Athens has, as its signature, that shining temple on a hill, it would indeed be hard to film scenes from the novel that take place on the Acropolis without being on site.

I thought quickly. "The point is not that he goes to Athens," I averred. "But that he goes to a big city where he succumbs to temptation. And, as they put it in the Bible, 'He ate up his substance with harlots.'"

The director agreed with me. "Town ways. Great sex scenes, big-city temptations."

The financier nodded. He poured himself scotch.

"Yeah, but which one?" asked Tweedle-Dum.

"Which city?" asked Tweedle-X.

Again, I thought quickly and said, "Istanbul." I'd never been to Istanbul and thought it might be picturesque or, at any rate, worth visiting. "It's just as easy to get to Turkey from Rhodes as it is to get to Athens. Why don't we set it there?"

The story editor knocked off cigar ash in the silver salver to his left. "Istanbul," he crowed. "Istanbul. I'm damn glad I thought of it."

"Yeah," said the executive producer. "It's the best idea I've had in *months*!"

"Terrific, kid," said the producer. "You're on."

They shot my story set in Greece, in Italy, and Tangiers.

Since that debut effort, I've published thirty books. Further, I've edited a dozen collections of the work of other authors and taught for fifty years. This means that the labor of my professional life had largely to do with language—my own, and that of predecessors and colleagues and students. While others handled bowls of soup or heavy construction machinery or microscopic surgical instruments or computer programs or herds of cattle or stacks of mail, I showed up for the job each dawn with—at least symbolically—a pen and sheet of paper. It's work that continues today.

My first novel was, as suggested above, a critical and commercial success—not reaching best-seller status but sufficient at the time to ensure that what I next wrote would be published. This came to pass. Yet through some impulse which now seems to me self-defining as well as self-defeating, my next two books were experimental and opaque. They were "very modern novels," as a critic for the *New York Times* averred, almost impossible of access and highly allusive and idiosyncratic. It was as if I tried to show whatever readership I might command that I had gone to college and earned an advanced degree. But I was an apprentice, still, and still in search of a voice.

Grasse, 3/23/66 began with the titular declaration with which some authors sign their last page: a record of the time and place of completed composition. It was an Orphic mystery, dealing with the mythic figure of Dionysus Zagreus and built out of fragments and puns and what I thought of as bon mots. As had been the case for the Bacchantes, his worshippers, the task of reconstructing the dismembered Dionysus was left suspended—almost as though its author tore narrative sequence apart. Set largely in the South of France, and conceived of as a love song, the book appeared in 1968.

Consider Sappho Burning, its successor next year, was an allegory of the senses—narrated by the "sixth" sense in occult communion with the other five; the speaker was a poet called

Aurore. The title derived from Lord Byron's "The isles of Greece / Where burning Sappho loved and sung . . ." I had planned to use that title for *The Martlet's Tale,* but my publishers objected that the name of Sappho would conjure up lesbian passion and mislead the market they hoped to attract. In the arrogance of youth—or perhaps just because I still liked the sound of *Consider Sappho Burning*—I wrote a novel of same-sex love and called it by that name.

In my next book, *News,* I moved to more public matters and tried to engage a political issue: the project of black separatism then everywhere discussed. It too was powered by a not-very-buried structure: the synoptic gospels. There were four contemporary disciples of an historical figure, Tunis G. Campbell Jr., whom they regarded as a kind of Christ. Once a hotel restaurant headwaiter in New York, Campbell briefly ruled a black kingdom on the Georgia Sea Islands, on the basis of General Sherman's Special Field Order #15, that each freedman should be granted "forty acres and a mule."

So there I was, at twenty-eight, the author of four novels and a film being edited in Rome. By almost any yardstick—except, perhaps, that of sales—I was an established writer and one who'd cut his eyeteeth in the guild. I don't mean to list each book of mine or rehearse its original intention—only to point to an early habit that became ingrained. The fifth book was a fictive autobiography, the sixth a blithe rehearsal of the *Oresteia,* the seventh a contemporary retelling of the tale of Tristan and Yseult. Always, it seemed, I needed a "backstory" from which to offer my variation on a theme; always I buttressed my own prose with a shadow-narrative on which I built the book. What strikes me now, a half-century later, is how confident I felt that there *would* be an audience, no matter how arcane the subject or highly worked the style.

Much of this certainty was enabled by the unwavering support of my then-editor, James ("Jim") Landis at William Morrow & Co. We met each other at La Toque Blanche, one of the restaurants I'd referred to in the manuscript of *Consider Sappho Burning*, and which Jim chose as the venue for our first encounter. I was impressed by the gesture—the attentive rigor of his reading, as well as the number of bottles of wine—and told my agent this was the fellow with whom I wished to sign. He was almost exactly my age, in his own way an enfant terrible of the trade, with a portfolio that would extend from Jaqueline Susann and rock stars to *Zen and the Art of Motorcycle Maintenance*—whose author, Robert Pirsig, became Jim's lifelong friend.

The young editor was everywhere, or so it seemed, and though we first met on professional terms he soon became an intimate, and we've remained that way. By the time of his retirement (a forced withdrawal from his post as publisher and editor-in-chief) we had published twelve books together, and I still think him a close colleague though he's no longer in the trade.

One of the by-blows of a long history of publication is that the writer begins to discern a pattern in his or her work. The reliance on urtexts referred to above has faded a little with time, though *The Years* (2015) was patterned on *The Winter's Tale*, and *Old Scores* (1997) was based on the letters of Abelard and Héloise. Now, more and more I dream my way into a novel or series of short stories without the benefit of a previous structure, and more and more I focus on the form of the tale to be told. I mean by this that the number of chapters and shape of the narrative claim my attention, whether or not the reader notices, and the self-generated story is a secondary thing. This is true of nonfiction as well; consider how these pages move in syncopated fashion between their several subjects—and how the word "consider" echoes the title of my book about a poet called Aurore.

Nowadays I'm one of those writers who's referred to as "distinguished." I once was "promising," and it took only fifty years to attain the adjective in the preceding sentence. To draw the line between true and false modesty is never easy, but I hope it not immodest to say the term "distinguished" partakes of condescension; it's how you categorize a person no longer in the game. The act of composition means much more to me by now than the reaction to it, and like any other habit it's harder to break than it once was to make. I get up every morning and sit to work by 6 a.m., and the body of language enlarges.

This morning, for example, Elena and I are en route to the east coast. We're in the Pocono Mountains, at an inn we've stayed in often where the dinners are substantial and the bed too soft. But we like it here, and it's something of a pivot point on our shared pilgrimage from Michigan to Massachusetts, if we travel between them by car. Outside there's a chill wintry dark, and since long before dawn I've been typing these lines. They're self-referential in a way my early work was not, but continuity offers comfort, and I wouldn't want to get behind the wheel without an hour or three at the desk.

In a preceding paragraph I used the phrase "the body of language enlarges." I puzzled, a bit, as to its accuracy and tried out some alternatives. "The trail of language continues" or "the body of discourse accumulates" might have served as well. I could have cut it altogether and ended the sentence with "6 a.m." Like almost every author, I wrote the five words five or six times and, when satisfied, moved on.

One of the yields of revision is the chance to make a line as perfect as its creator can manage. In no other mode of expression do we get an equivalent chance. (Composers and painters rework their original versions as well, but my focus here is on the written word.) In conversation or even lecture mode we permit ourselves errata: small inaccuracies of imagery or diction, shortcuts or half-formed phrases that nonetheless serve their turn. But, when writing, one tries hard to get terminology right. And in that sense the phrase I used is precisely the one I intended, since the weight of a "body of language" does feel corporeal. Too, the process of revision for a writer partakes of that strange sacrament called transubstantiation, from first to final draft.

Max Eastman was in his eighties when I was in my twenties. We met on Martha's Vineyard and grew close. He welcomed me, whether in Gay Head, New York, or Barbados; he was tolerance incarnate, with an amused abiding sense of how youth preens. In addition to his work as activist and editor, he had published more than twenty books—volumes of poetry, biography, and political commentary, as well as a set of translations from the Russian; the second installment of his autobiography, *Love and Revolution: My Journey through an Epoch* (1964) seemed a title entirely earned.

As suggested above, my second book (*Grasse 3/23/66*) was recondite in the extreme. I'd labor in an ecstasy of self-congratulation, producing perhaps a hundred words a day, intoning the sibilant syllables until they appeared to make sense. One such passage, I remember, contained a quotation from Villon; a description of Hopi burial rites; an anagram of the name of my fifth-grade teacher; an irrefutable refutation of Kant; a glancing reference to Paracelsus; suggestive ditto to my agent's raven-haired assistant; paraphrase of Cymbeline's dirge; and an analysis of the orthographic and conceptual distinction between Pope and Poe.

I took my time; I let it extend to ten lines. That night I brought my morning's triumph to Max and permitted him to read. He did so in silence. Then he tried it aloud; so did I. When he said it made no sense and I explained the sense it made, he looked at me with fond exasperation. "Sure," he said. "That's interesting. Why don't you write it down?"

I remember staying with him on Martha's Vineyard one October. His wife, Yvette, was off to New York for a shopping trip, and she asked me to sleep in their house—a favor to me, really, since my own hut was unheated. I was full of beans and bravado, and would get to work by six—waking up and clacking at the keys in my upstairs bedroom. In the first pause, however, I could hear his steady hunt-and-peck in the study underneath; he'd been at work well before. So we'd share a cup of coffee and a comment on the news, then I'd fuss at my novel again. At nine o'clock I'd take a break—tear off my clothes and run down the hill to the pond. The morning would be glorious: that crystalline light, those sizeable skies, the pine trees somehow greener against the sere scrub oak. And always, out there in the still warm water, Max would lift his hand to me, his white mane on the wavelets like some snowy egret's, grinning.

Time passed. He died at eighty-six, in 1969. But it takes no effort to see this again: an old man waving from the water at a youth on the near shore. They are naked, both of them; the sun slants over Lobsterville. A few day sailors might be on the pond, or someone in a kayak, or musseling or digging clams. Gulls drift past, incurious; the beach smells of sea-wrack and weed. There's a busy imitation of silence: the man in the water, bobbing, flutters heels and hands. The young one runs to meet him and it's all a perfect clarity until he does a surface dive and, splashing, shuts his eyes.

For some years in the late 1970s and early 1980s the very notion of professional identity was, for me, collective. Though now beyond full retrieval, the gathering of writers—novelists, short story writers, journalists, and poets—who came to Bennington stays vivid to me still. The late John Gardner and I conceived of a summer writing workshop as a context for developing texts—as opposed, say, to the model of the Breadloaf Writers' Conference, where participants would bring in finished texts for critique. Our students were to start afresh or hand in new drafts of their work, not wait to be commended for what they had earlier written. We designed the Bennington Summer Writing Workshops to last a month, though with an option for two-week stays, and—to begin with, at least—relied on friendships to fill out the faculty ranks.

By now there's a certain "been there, done that" feel to such gatherings, and the tedium of repeated experience. You can't throw a rock in New England without hitting a writers' conference, and there are "workshop junkies" addicted to making the rounds. Back then, though, few if any authors refused an invitation, and soon enough our roster of literary luminaries became a kind of honor guard, a group people hurried to join. In the first five years, our list of invitees included Lisa Alther, Rosellen Brown, Frederick Buechner, Hortense Calisher, John Cheever, Ralph Ellison, Louise Glück, John Irving, Jamaica Kincaid, Carolyn Kizer, Maxine Kumin, Bernard Malamud, David McCullough, Joe McGinniss, Ved Mehta, Bharati Mukherjee, Joyce Carol Oates, Grace Paley, Robert Pinsky, Anne Roiphe, Mary Lee Settle, Ted Solotaroff, John Updike, Ellen Bryant Voigt, Jay Wright, and too many more to name. In the span of time I directed the program, (1977–1985) nearly two-hundred writers joined us in Vermont.

One of our central tenets was an equivalence of treatment, so that first-time authors and grandees received the same payment—an honorarium of two hundred dollars, which even then was notional. Over time the fee enlarged to an extravagant two hundred and fifty dollars. There was also, of course, the chance to stay on the picturesque campus and revel in the Green Mountains and the local streams and pastures in July. (John Cheever, I remember, returned his honorarium, as did many others, refusing to be, for such company, paid.) Each visitor spent the same amount of time at a shared podium; each panel discussion was comprised of apprentices and recognized artists, without hierarchical rank. In this way apprentice authors such as Bret

Easton Ellis, Mary Ruefle, Mona Simpson, and David Foster Wallace took center stage along with their elders, and the spirit of collective effort was very much in play.

Another kind of "spirit" was everywhere in evidence; I can remember William Kennedy and Thomas Flanagan working their way through two bottles of scotch in one evening at our house. Madison Smartt Bell, George Booth, Blanche Boyd, John Darnton, Stephen Dunn, Mary and Jim Robison, Lee Smith, Arturo Vivante, Hilma Wolitzer, and Al Young all graced the table, drinking and singing and smoking, telling jokes and telling lies. Annie Dillard, Betty Friedan, and Norman Lear flew in. Richard Bausch, Richard Eberhart, Richard Ford, Richard Howard, and Richard Wilbur each stood at the podium; editors and agents and publishers from New York and Boston came to our corner of rural Vermont to speak about components of the trade. I'm aware that all this is mere summary and dull as a recounting of someone else's party, with its list of soon-to-be-forgotten notables. But at the time the dead were quick, and those of us who now grow old were young.

Elena was the hostess for the whole. Our house served from the start as the focal point for visitor gatherings; she cooked routinely for a dozen and sometimes, on weekends, for seventy-five. Our mandate from Bennington College was to break even (and fill the empty campus), not to make a profit. Accordingly, we spent large sums on entertainment, and even if those revels are now ended they remain, in memory, lightsome and laughter-filled. Faculty members such as Susan Richards Shreve and Dave Smith arrived with their young families, and there was a gaggle of children, always, in the fields. The nearby lake and tennis courts were chockablock with what I liked to call "typists," and though there were some dissatisfied students and a spate of brief or failed romances, my overarching memory is of the serious good humor of it all.

Two colleagues were central to our gatherings. The first was the poet, short story writer, and novelist George Garrett, the second the fiction writer and journalist Alan Cheuse. Both, alas, are gone: George at the age of seventy-nine in 2008 and Alan in a car crash in 2015. The former died at home in Charlottesville, Virginia, the latter on the road to Santa Cruz, California. Both of these regular faculty members—along with the much-mourned Anglo-Welsh author Jon Manchip White—embody the spirit of place. The ring of high-pitched hilarity or impassioned argument sounds in my ear resoundingly long after their voices went mute.

I have never known a man so generous of spirit as George Garrett, so unstintingly supportive of his acolytes and students. Not possible to pay for a meal if George were in the restaurant, not possible to count the number of bottles he brought to the house or bouquets for Elena. His Elizabethan trilogy—*Death of the Fox, The Succession,* and *Entered from the Sun*—still seems to me a masterful achievement, yet he wore his learning lightly and was gracious to a fault. The quizzical smile, the soft southern inflection, the glinting ribaldry and low muttering chuckle have disappeared, but the books remain.

Alan Cheuse was also crucial: an omnivorous reader and tireless writer, best known perhaps as the book reviewer for NPR's *All Things Considered.* He came to the practice of prose fiction late, or relatively so, having acquired a doctorate in comparative literature, and writing on the great Cuban Alejo Carpentier. Convivial yet exacting, he was a beloved teacher and—like George—unstinting in his sponsorship of other authors. Always, he asked me, "What are you reading?" and would commend a new book.

Many of the writers I've named—Calisher, Cheuse, Gardner, Garrett, for instance—I tried to hire so they could keep teaching at the college during the academic year. For one reason or another, the long-term arrangements failed to work out, and the term-time yield of colleagueship was, by comparison, scant. But the month-long gatherings of the Bennington Summer Writing Workshops seem emblematic still of what a shared circle offers, and how the presence of an admired friend and fellow traveler invigorates one's own engagement with the work of words.

A further memory. Each summer the King Brothers Circus came to the town of Bennington, performing for two or three days. It was a seedy traveling troupe, but they had the full regalia of a Little Big Top: painted trucks and clowns and jugglers and tightrope walkers and dogs and ponies and, to raise the tent, three elephants. These troupers bedded down in the rear fields of the college, not far from one of the faculty houses where Alan Cheuse and his two daughters lodged. When, in September, he moved to Knoxville, Tennessee, and enrolled his children in the local preschool, the teacher asked the entering students where they had been and what they had done for the summer. Alan's elder daughter, Emma, said she watched the elephants outside her bedroom window—and, that afternoon, when her father came to collect her, the teacher took him aside.

"Your child has quite the imagination, Mr. Cheuse," she said. "But should you let her make things up, oh, what's the word? *Brazenly*? Elephants in Vermont?"

I don't know if he told her his daughter was telling the truth.

In Bennington, those summers, there were wonders in the fields.

Another faculty member belonged to that party. Richard Elman (1934–1997) was an important figure in literary circles of the latter part of the last century, a consequential presence in our culture's "scene." Known primarily as a novelist—for such novels as *The Reckoning* (1969) and *An Education in Blood* (1971)—he was also a social commentator, with such nonfiction books as *Ill-at-Ease in Compton* (1967) and *Uptight with the Stones: A Novelist's Report* (1973). He worked for New York's left-leaning radio station WBAI; he wrote the novelization of the movie *Taxi Driver* (1976); he traveled to Nicaragua for *Cocktails at Somoza's* (1981). Further, his pseudonymous *Little Lives* (1978) and his posthumously published *Namedropping* (1998) were widely reviewed and well received. Beginning with his study *The Poorhouse State: The American Way of Life on Public Assistance* (1966) and ending with the surrealistic novel *Tar Beach* (1991), he produced a steady stream—a torrent, really—of prose.

But Elman thought of himself, first and foremost, as a poet. Poetry was his great love. He published it in such collections as *The Man Who Ate New York* (1975), *Homage to Fats Navarro* (1978), *In Chontales* (1980), and *Cathedral Tree-Train and Other Poems* (1992). There were chapbooks and smaller collections as well, showing a constant commitment to the form; his devotion to the genre stayed with him till he died. An omnibus volume of his verse, edited by his widow, Alice Goode-Elman, has recently appeared.

I met Richard in the late 1960s, when we taught together at Bennington College and became, rapidly, friends. He was walking up a hill.

"Are you that Delbanco I just read about?" were his first words to me. "The one who comes from Italy?"

"Came from Italy," I said.

"But you were born there?"

"No. In England."

"Your cousins are the Warburgs, right? They were part of your family way back when."

"Not really. Well, four hundred years ago."

"I've also got cousins," he said, "in Brooklyn and New Jersey. Welcome to the tribe."

In Vermont the writer cut a wide swathe—briefly as a term-time teacher and then as a member of the faculty of the Bennington Summer Writing Workshops, which he joined early on. But when I hired him as a visiting professor at the University of Michigan, some years later, his sensibility was as oil in water. Elman's New York abruptness did not mix with Midwestern good manners. On the first day of the semester, he walked into the seminar space holding a sheaf of student stories. There was a microwave oven for the use of faculty members in a corner of the room. Richard walked to it, opened it, put the pages in and pressed some numbers, then *Start.*

"This is what we do with half-baked manuscripts," he said.

Although he slouched and lumbered, our "Richele" was large—about six-three, and wide. For a period he lived in the same apartment building as the violinist Mischa Elman, who was no relation, a foot shorter, and concertized in dress clothes. These elegant garments—sometimes a tuxedo or white jacket, sometimes tails—would need to be cleaned after a few performances. Routinely, they were returned by mistake, pressed and gleaming, not to the diminutive violinist but to the great galoot upstairs. He told me, more in anger than sorrow, that they failed to fit.

Another such failure of "suitability" came many years later, when Richard was a visiting faculty member in the writing program at the University of Pennsylvania. His time as a teacher had expired and, leafing through the university's announcements of available positions for the next semester, he saw that they were searching for a new dean of the dental school. This is a paraphrase of what he wrote, but accurate:

> It's true I've never been a dentist or attended Medical School. But I have some administrative experience and I know the only three things a dentist needs to say.
>
> 1. Open wide
> 2. This won't hurt much.
> 3. Please pay at the door.

For most of us, this would have been a joke and sent in the spirit of fun. Yet why I loved my wacky friend was that he took umbrage with the dental school for failing to interview and take him seriously. His *amour propre* was fragile, his mood swings precipitous, his exaltations intense. In the technical sense he was bipolar—when happy, elated, when sad, abject—and it was never easy to predict which Richard Elman would walk through the door. In the depths of his depression, once, he committed himself to Bellevue; at the height of his exuberance, he wrote eighteen hours a day. Lithium or Prozac were both needful and anathema; he couldn't write, he told me, when made peaceful by mood-altering drugs—and he'd wean himself from them for the spurt-spate of a book.

I dedicated to him one of my own: *Group Portrait: Joseph Conrad, Stephen Crane, Ford Madox Ford, Henry James, and H. G. Wells* (1982). It was subtitled "A Study of Writers in Community," and my dedication read: "To Richard Elman. Who has represented, from the first, the collegiality this book proposes." The eminent English biographer and critic Victoria Glendinning reviewed *Group Portrait* favorably but chastised me for having been careless with the spelling of my dedicatee. She said, in effect, that in a book so otherwise exact and exacting I should have spelled the name of the biographer of Joyce and Wilde correctly. It's true that Richard Ellmann has a separate orthography, but he was not the man I meant to praise and thank. Even at the height of his renown, therefore, Richard Elman was misprized; the tuxedo failed to fit.

In any account of my friendships, he deserves a central place. We spoke to each other weekly, often daily; we taught together, shared family triumphs and troubles; we read each other's work-in-progress, laughed at each other's jokes, and blurbed each other's books. We stayed close until the end.

One summer night in Vermont, I remember, an eclipse of the moon was predicted to take place. There was a party in our house, much revelry, and at the given moment Richard walked out to the meadow and lay down in the wet tall grass, pointing upwards, urging us to join him. "You can see it better here," he shouted. "The moon's much closer, everybody. Everyone, come on!"

I published my first novel in 1966; I began to teach that same year. The arithmetic is easy—fifty-seven years have gone by—the recognition hard. My face was one I used to scrutinize; now it's a reflection I try to avoid. Instead, I find myself more and more often reflecting on the lost look of things past.

These last two words echo my oft-quoted Shakespeare's "remembrance of things past," and that phrase was used by C. K. Scott Moncrieff in his translation of Proust's *À la Recherche du Temps Perdu*. It is a second meaning of the one word, "reflection," that comes to mind; what I see in the mirror mirrors both a present face and its long-previous guise. Where once I used to fantasize on future encounters, romantic or professional, I now rehearse what went before and will not come again.

This is a common pattern in the elderly: Our short-term memory may falter but the distant memory is readily retrieved. "What's past is prologue," as the playwright elsewhere writes, but it's also and irredeemably the case that what's past is past. The name of a friend or colleague or lover from 1966 is—or so I tell myself—set in stone, but the name of the person across last night's table is not one I retain. This lapse can be explained in terms of the brain's chemistry, but it comes as a shock nonetheless to be certain of what happened on that July day and night when my first book was published, and to forget—or remember at best hazily—what transpired in July this year.

When I and my then-colleagues commenced on a career, it was with the assumption that the career would last. The hope was for enlargement, the fear, of diminution, but it never occurred to me or my compatriots that publication was a one-off and not to be repeated. Now, in America, it's "Here today and gone tomorrow," and soon enough the phrase may be "Here and gone today." If I enact the role of Old Father Time and harrumph about the change, it's with a sense of *temps perdu* as well as present circumstance; my first publishers had hoped that early success would expand and increase but were in it—or so they assured me—for the long haul.

Those times antedated the computer, with its ability to track the sales of a book almost on the instant; sales records were an abstract thing, not immediately germane to an editorial decision as to whether or not to acquire a book. Then the judgment was taste-based at least as much as number-driven, and the personal reaction of an editor or publisher counted as much as receipts. Now it feels as though the midlist author is an endangered species, and it's in some sense better to be a beginner than a proven entity.

Each month a star is born and every month another fades or fails. I can remember telling people, when my first book appeared, that I knew I'd be writing ten years thence but had no idea of the subject or form; I had embarked on a profession but did not know where it would lead. That it *would* lead to further publication was, however, my near-certainty; such confidence today might be ill-advised.

Therefore, these lines focus on the presence of the past. *What Remains* is a novel that appeared in the year 2000; two decades later I published a novel called—no doubt appropriately —*It Is Enough.* Both these titular phrases sound, at least to their author, elegiac. "What thou lovest well remains," as Ezra Pound declared, "The rest is dross." Now more and more I come to see that the note of elegy has been central to my prose. The key is minor, the tempo slow, and the compositions often as not confined to single movements, not three or four or five. I have, I've come to understand, been haunted by those wistful formulations: *If only* or *On second thought* or *What might have been.*

"Heureux qui, comme Ulysse, a fait un beau Voyage." This phrase from Joachim du Bellay, in the mid-sixteenth century, has special resonance for me; it was uttered often by my beloved friend and colleague Jon Manchip White (1924–2013). "Happy the man who, like Ulysses, has made a fair voyage"—or, less formally, "good trip." When looking back near the end of his career Jon did so smilingly, not ruefully, setting a stoic's example of how to deal with decline.

The choice to revisit a life lived ill or well is almost inescapable—all the more so as we age. This seems doubly the case if the life is the life of a writer. Very few authors escape an autobiographical impulse at some point in their career, and almost all indulge themselves in retrospect. How else can we continue than in the vein we opened and mined for our professional life? Childhood and parental (mis)behavior and first romance and love and loss all become grist for the mill. Soon or late we come to paraphrase Descartes's dictum: *Cogito, ergo sum.* In the professional author's parlance, it's "I write, therefore I am."

Still Life at Eighty is no exception to what I here claim as the general rule. There have been bits and snatches of experience dispersed throughout my work; how could this not be so? I was never—or never consciously—a proponent of confessional fiction, but the novels and short stories are rife with characters encountered, places visited, conversations overheard. Only the most extreme of fantasists—those who write historical or science fiction, say—can avoid mining a private life lived, and those who wish to hunt for clues to personal experience will find, here, fertile ground. Now more and more, my novels deal with personal history: an aging author's catalogue of how and where he lived in times and places gone by. It's a form of armchair travel and "remembrance of things past."

In the spring of 2023 I sat in Winston Churchill's chair, where he labored in the darkest days of war. Variously known as the Churchill War Rooms, or the Cabinet War Rooms, in London, the venue belongs to the collective entity called the Imperial War Museum (IWM), which sponsors five separate sites. Membership entitles you to view such displays as the HMS *Belfast* and the air show at Duxford, but the War Rooms are the collection's crown jewel and—to shift the metaphor—its still-beating heart. The Second World War plays a central part in our collective consciousness, and those who visit Normandy (or, in our country, Gettysburg) will travel here as well.

Churchill held conference far underground, in an otherwise nondescript building on King Charles Street in Whitehall. His cabinet members and advisers joined him "belowstairs," as did personnel manning the phones. Access was closely monitored and those who gained entry were few. The furnishings are spare. Layers of protective concrete were poured above the meeting rooms; there are no windows, and the air would no doubt have reeked with smoke. I can't conjure up the smells of sweat or fearful concentration, but they would have been part of the mix. The cramped space has the feel of a bunker, a place to escape from in order to breathe open air.

Yet it has been preserved. The restoration of the War Rooms has been reverential. We were in London—as were, by coincidence, our older daughter and her California family, who had booked a tour. According to the guide, these are the very pencils and file folders and blotters and inkwells and ashtrays that were then in use (though I doubt the flaking ash-tipped cigars were puffed on during sessions some eighty years ago.) The meeting room contains the original four-sided table and, around it, the same chairs. In an adjacent office, the color-coded telephones and maps (with pins in them to position ships and troops and enemy encampments) seem just as they once were. There's a black electric fan on the wall; clocks continue to monitor time.

On August 27, 1939—three years to the day before I was born—the War Rooms went operational. Their address was, for obvious reasons, kept top secret, and the rooms were used with regularity—on 115 separate occasions—during the course of the war. Routinely, the discussions took place in the midst of V-weapon attacks and the Luftwaffe's Blitz. Churchill took shelter here with his cabinet and chief military officers, most if not all of them male. The typists, stenographers, and switchboard operators were female and, if told to spend the night, consigned to what was called "the dock."

Security would have been tight. Since the prime minister hated distraction, the Remington typewriters used by his staff were specially fitted to be noiseless. Wartime rationing was strict; when, in the early1980s, these rooms were prepared for public display, workers found three sugar cubes in an envelope hidden in a drawer of a Map Room desk. The officer with his name on the envelope—Wing Commander John Heagerty—would have secreted a private supply, and his sugar cubes stayed intact.

To counteract depression and the lack of light, all personnel were told to strip down to their underclothes and stand daily for some minutes in front of a sun lamp. There are many such accounts of wartime protocol, but the secondary cots and washrooms and the kitchen were not what we went underground to see.

Glass doors shield the inner space from tour groups passing by. But Francesca and her husband—with their Hollywood contacts—had secured a private tour. We were conducted through the building by its retired director, a white-haired affable fellow proud of his list of previous visitors (Bill Clinton and Harrison Ford among them) and his OBE. Extracting a key from his pocket, then bending down to unlock the glass partitions, he ushered us inside. We entered the sanctum sanctorum and I sat in Churchill's chair.

In front of the prime minister's place a red leather dispatch box awaits his close attention. There's an ashtray and a paperweight and an array of pens. But there's no webbing or cushion for the actual seat he sat on; it's been sent out for repair. Sitting at the head of the conference table, I had to straddle emptiness and stare out at a vacant space where the warrior once made his battle plans.

Churchill was restless, impatient. The right arm of the heavy chair is battered where he pounded it to make a rhetorical point; the left has been emblazoned by scratch-marks of his ring. Often, in spite of his subordinates' pleading, he would stand on the building's open balcony to survey the damage caused by bombs; he slept on his cot only rarely, and the bed pan at the foot of his bed shows no evidence of use. But it takes small imagination to place his bulky body on the dark bentwood chair once more, or to hear the plummy accent and the stentorian voice. He wrote and delivered speeches in and from this place; he kept his cognac and, we were told, bananas in a private cabinet. Whenever he wanted he blustered his way past the protesting guards and went upstairs to watch the war.

For this Jewish son of German refugees, Hitler's assault on London was a matter of literal life and death. I did not understand this when a child, of course, but in the Cabinet War Rooms I was assailed by memory: the taste of rationed chocolate, the hedgehog scuttling rapidly through long grass to our garden's edge, my mother, my older brother, the fog. Our father had festooned the walls of the stone garage in which we slept with images of elephants and donkeys and giraffes; the paintings offered nighttime comfort to me then and do so now in hindsight. My children and grandchildren would not have taken form without the long-dead formless shape of the embattled prime minister in this echoic space.

Had he not been defiant, the *Anschluss* would have proved unstoppable, and my family would not have survived. Sitting there in Churchill's chair, I felt the past and present and the future fuse.

PART III

Things of this World

Autobiography as genre is hydra-headed today. It doesn't require previous prominence; it can be written by someone escaped from a small town in Appalachia or the stifling confines of privilege or marriage or religion. These are privacies made public which once were held close to the vest. A common denominator of such stories—almost an organizing principle of the contemporary memoir—is that a "home truth" comes to be told, and the more shocking the better.

Whether produced in a palace, library, or prison cell, we read the "tell-all" tale. We readers learn of fraud, abuse, incest, sexual addiction, double-agenting, criminal parents, ancestral outrage, pride, disguised identity, self-mutilation, and so on. A memoir is most often selective; it reports on a specific set of incidents and people. An autobiography is extensive and inclusive, but the confessional mode structures both. A well-known name is not requisite here; indeed, the reverse can be true, and often the "I" of the story is Anon.

Consider such tales as John Cleland's *Fanny Hill: Memoirs of a Woman of Pleasure* (1748), or Laurence Sterne's *The Life and Opinions of Tristram Shandy, Gentleman* (1798): first-person texts purporting to be autobiographical but by some other author composed. These histories are fiction. Yet as soon as we write "I"—no matter how spurious or invented the pronoun—we claim some of the immediacy of a diary or trip-log or letter. All first-person novels (think of *David Copperfield* or *Jane Eyre*) strive for authenticity (even when the narrator is "nontrust-worthy"), but fictional truth telling is not my subject here. Neither Charles Dickens nor Charlotte Brontë believed themselves confessional when publishing first-person tales.

Nor is it necessarily the case that the "I" of autobiography be an authentic or unmediated one. Some memoirs are wholly fabricated; others are in part inexact; most often, it's a mixture of the two. Why should I believe Lord Russell's assertion that he can remember what his nanny told him when he was four years old (because it's reported in *The Autobiography of Bertrand Russell*) or disbelieve the novelist Marcel Proust's reconstruction of overheard speech when he was the same age?

Most often, autobiography is couched in retrospect and details a public career. "My life as a soldier, as a politician, as a movie star or business mogul or model or scientist or athlete"—these tales are omnipresent, and the more famous the subject the larger the audience. Routinely, beans are spilled for millions of dollars once the writer is no longer constrained to silence or restraint. To leave the White House is to enter a publisher's office; to retire from the FBI or CIA is to embark—once the manuscript has been vetted—on a publicity tour.

Such retrospectives are often "ghost written" or "as told to" a professional author; thus, a kind of second self is involved. *The Autobiography of Malcolm X*, to take a salient example, was composed by Alex Haley and based on tape recordings after Malcolm's death. Notable singers or generals or athletes need not be accomplished as writers to have their stories told and experience enshrined. My Life in *X* or *Y* or *Z* does not require that the "my" be an actual first-person account, and the line between biography and autobiography is often hard to draw.

Therefore, when a public personality uses personal language—think of the memoirs of Ulysses S. Grant or books composed by Barack Obama—we readers are doubly impressed. They stand almost as exceptions to the rule. There's a subset of the genre—including *The Autobiography of Alice B. Toklas*, written by Gertrude Stein, as well as campaign declarations and retrospectives of a career—that are only rarely self-generated prose.

But whether written by the actual author or by a "ghost" writer or an "as-told-to" scribe, the navel-gazing stance persists. *My side of the story* is, by definition, the operational mode. Most often, these accounts are self-serving, not self-flagellating; the attempt to "set the record straight" is a main engine of the genre.

Intention matters here. Some autobiographies are meant to be confessional; others try instead to justify behavior and polish a portrait detractors have drawn. Some are hagiographies; others describe "the chief of sinners" and castigate the self. *Apologia pro Vita Sua*, John Henry Newman's spiritual treatise (1864), is an assertion of faith. Thomas De Quincy's *Confessions of an Opium Eater* (1821) deals at length with matters other than that of its titular topic—yet the title, or so I imagine, keeps the book current today.

Some authors report on glad companions or great deeds witnessed; they bask in the reflected glory of associates (My

Life with *A*, My Mother *B*, My Cousin *C*., etc.). Others write of failure and lifelong anonymity, but if they do it well enough the failure and the anonymity will be dispensed with by text's end. Some deal with lengthy life and offer up a final vantage on what went before; others deal with early sorrow or a mid-life crisis and suggest that things will change.

But whether it's Life of the Sinner or Life of the Saint, the generative impulse is the same. Vladimir Nabokov rewrote his autobiography, first published as *Conclusive Evidence* in 1951. His revised and enlarged version, *Speak Memory*, came out in 1966, with the subtitle "An Autobiography Revisited." His publishers endorsed that qualifier, though they apparently objected to his initial hope to title it, "Speak, Mnemosyne," in honor of the muse who governs recollection. As any raconteur will know, an anecdote takes shape—assuming form and cadence —with only minor variations over time. A cocktail party or a courtroom may occasion the same story, and context matters in the nature of such speech. Yet even as the arena of exposition alters, we want our stories told.

More than twenty years ago I wrote an essay titled, "A Prayer for the Daughters." I took as my springboard the poem "A Prayer for my Daughter," by William Butler Yeats. His great first stanza opens with these lines:

> Once more the storm is howling, and half hid
> Under this cradle-hood and coverlid
> My child sleeps on.

My wife and I have two daughters, and they were then young women and as yet unwed. Now both of them are married parents in their forties, and living lives elsewhere. My own experience of childhood was as a son who had two brothers; the father-son relationship was therefore one I found familiar, but a father-daughter interaction was, for this writer, new. As its title suggests, "A Prayer . . ." deals with that new circumstance and the hard-won knowledge that, as the poet puts it, "Hearts are not had as a gift but hearts are earned."

The wheel turns. As productive adults, our daughters have careers I honor in the world of words. Francesca published a novel, *Ask Me Anything* (2004), that was widely praised; now she's a writer and director with two television series under her belt, the first for Netflix, the second for Apple TV. Andrea is the editor-in-chief of *TIME for Kids* and, as vice president of education, responsible for *Time* magazine's initiatives for children, families, and educators. Both have achieved success in their professions but not—as far as I can tell—at the expense of their personal lives. Each seems happily married (one for nineteen years, one, eighteen) and both flourish as proud mothers of daughters of their own. When we gather now at table, the clan numbers eleven. It's a familiar arithmetic—our "nuclear" four, two sons-in-law, and five young girls who call themselves "the cousins' club" and huddle together in corners to whisper and cackle and laugh.

Our sons-in-law are men I like and admire—one a major "player" in the entertainment industry (as screenwriter, director, producer), one a senior supervising attorney and director of supreme court advocacy for the New Jersey ACLU. Our daughters' daughters—three on the west coast, two on the east—range in age from sixteen to seven years old. I love these children and find them each remarkable, so I'm the very definition of a doting father and grandfather. What I hoped for in that early essay has, by and large, come true.

Though I know these lines from 2000 appear time-worn and conditioned by tradition, I wrote:

> Yes, I want my daughters to walk at some point down some aisle on my arm—though I don't require them to wear white or be married in a building that has aisles. Yes, I want them to be happy in the way their parents have been, and to emulate as women that exemplary woman who nurtured them throughout their youth and continues to do so today. I recognize that married love is neither original nor, perhaps, now fashionable—but it has made their father happy for nearly thirty years. And what I hope for them is not something other or contrary but, rather, more of the same.

The "nearly thirty years" can now be changed to "more than fifty," and indeed there's been "more of the same." I recognize that Elena and I and our children have been wildly fortunate, and a superstitious part of me has qualms about such summaries, for fear they may sound boastful. We all are fortune's fools. To be happy and successful is not to rest assured those conditions will continue; the wheel continues to turn. There's no guarantee good luck will hold, and the reason I come back to this topic and that title has much to do with the world's weather, for "once more the storm is howling."

The last two lines of the first stanza of Yeats's poem read: "And for an hour I have walked and prayed / Because of the great gloom that is in my mind." Any sentient citizen today must be full of forebodings and "gloom"; the world we at present inhabit is more troubled and at risk than the one in which I wrote at the turn of the millennium: Terrorism, climate change, pandemics, the proliferation of nuclear weapons, oppression and inequality are part of a long list of troubles that make Yeats's plaint seem tame.

The poet was unhappy that "fine women eat / A crazy salad with their meat," but this was more a function of his disappointed love for Maud Gonne than concerns about gender identity or sexual harassment or—as in our present headlines—slavery and rape. When he wrote of "custom" and "ceremony" he was using code words for a certain kind of social interaction that now seems antiquated if not antediluvian, and those very words—*antiquated, antediluvian*—belong to a form of discourse that's dying if not dead. When our recent president can shout that an opponent "kissed the ass" of his predecessor, and be applauded for saying, of women, "you can grab them by the pussy," we're part of a behavior pattern Yeats abhorred, and which he greatly feared. The more abrasive the better is the rule for candidates for office, and falsehood has cornered the market on truth. "In courtesy I'd have her chiefly learned," Yeats wrote, and what he meant by "courtesy" is more than mere good manners: a courtly recognition of custom which should be honored, not breached.

In "The Second Coming," Yeats wrote, "The best lose all conviction, while the worst / Are full of passionate intensity," and this remains the case. Our politicians are vulgar, hate-filled, shrill; our people turn to automatic weapons and incendiary bombs. The civil discourse engaged in by our Founding Fathers seems increasingly outmoded; intransigence is not the exception but the rule. Donald J. Trump describes his political opponents as a "lynch mob" or "human scum," and the tone deaf excess of his accusation is just one of the thousand ways "a passionate intensity" has come to stain our speech.

So a "great gloom" feels warranted, and a prayer for the daughters and the daughters' daughters is born out of fear and not faith. That child beneath the "cradle-hood and coverlid" seems more and more at risk.

In my own youth—the late 1940s and the early 1950s—the sense that people needed to "hide and take cover" was everywhere endemic. After the horrors of Hiroshima and Nagasaki and the ensuing proliferation of nuclear weapons, we were told as schoolchildren to prepare for an attack by diving under our desks. There were drills on a regular basis; there were community fallout shelters and programs for private construction of these putatively safe havens; there was a national conviction that everyone had to get ready for radiation's assault. Signs for air raid shelters spawned on subway platforms and sidewalks. Herman Kahn's *Thinking About the Unthinkable* was a near-required text.

The first house I described in these pages sat "in the middle of nowhere" in rural upstate New York. It was far from a grocery store or bank, surrounded by hills and pastures: unimaginable as a target for enemy attack. But it was roughly thirty miles from a General Electric plant, which might have been a target, and then-governor Nelson Rockefeller urged his constituents to stock up on water and canned goods and blankets in order to survive nuclear war. So the two-hundred-year-old house had its own cement-block structure in the basement, built by a previous owner to government specifications, protecting the spiders and mice.

In retrospect this all seems mad, as if radioactive fallout could be countered by a wooden or a metal desk and a bomb shelter with tin cans of soup. But at the time we lived with the near-constant fear of catastrophe: a nuclear clock set seconds before midnight while Armageddon approached. It's in a certain sense remarkable that nearly eighty years have passed since the first use of atomic bombs deployed against a populace. And we're a little less fearful by now—though Russia's megalomaniacal leader, Vladimir Putin, has raised the specter once again—of nuclear annihilation and a Third World War. We know a good deal more today than in the 1950s about the awful aftermath of a mushroom cloud.

Still, the image of children practicing their safety drill is not easy to dismiss, and in Syria and Yemen and the Ukraine and Israel while the rockets and grenades explode, it remains a governing image of innocence under assault. All over the world—in China, Myanmar, Palestine, Mali, Haiti—the hunted and the haunted crouch beneath their desks.

Our granddaughter Frederica has a different take on things. She told us, beaming, when last year a coast guard helicopter flew above us at the beach, that she gets lollipops. "Oh good," she crowed and pointed, "This means treats." I asked her what she meant, and she explained that—in her school in Los Angeles, when a helicopter hovers overhead—her teachers herd everybody into a classroom closet and turn off the lights. "If we stay very quiet," she said, "when we come out again we all get lollipops." This well-managed response to the threat of mass shooting is a safety drill each school feels compelled to engage in, and it deals with a more immediate horror than did fallout shelters, but the effort is much the same: Make of survival a game.

Another memory. I was a senior in college in the fall of 1962, when what became known as the Cuban Missile Crisis captured the world's attention. I was preparing a student production of Federico Garcia Lorca's *Blood Wedding*, a play I would direct at the Loeb Drama Center in Cambridge. As we embarked upon our "tech and costume rehearsal," two nights before our scheduled opening, President Kennedy addressed the nation from the White House. It was October 22. We gathered in the Green Room of the newly opened theater—roughly thirty Harvard undergraduates comprising the cast and the technical crew—to listen to and watch the speech. His was a telegenic presence, and he was a good performer, but there was no mistaking the gravity of what he said and threatened: all-out war.

I can remember looking at the actors in their costumes but without makeup, which made them more pallid by contrast while we sat awaiting our fate. All of us were of draft age and many of us male. When the speech was over we debated if we should continue or abandon the project—since the likelihood of an opening night, two nights thereafter, seemed slim. At length we decided "the show must go on" and prepared for the performance, which did in fact take place. But in a marginally more adult fashion, I felt like that second-grader crouched under a desk and hoping for the siren to announce, "All clear." It's not easy today to recapture the sense of dread that beleaguered us then, and to which we grew accustomed: The planet and our very existence all seemed at imminent risk.

Those were immediate not long-term fears; the reverse is now the case. Most of my contemporaries think we ourselves will survive "global warming," and the threatened extinction of numerous species does not yet include Homo sapiens. Sea levels rise and glaciers melt, but some other islanders must flee their sea-submerged dwellings, and polar bears still flourish in the nation's zoos. It's our children and our children's children who seem more likely to suffer annihilation; we'll squeak by through our remaining years, perhaps, but they won't be as fortunate while the planet's weather shifts.

It's not an accident that the at-least-symbolic leaders of activism on climate change are young people—teenagers, even—and a Swedish girl, Greta Thunberg, became the movement's spokesperson. They are the ones who'll suffer and pay the price of their parents' inattention; they are the generation who will inherit this wind. "*Après moi, le déluge*," as the King of France famously said, but the deluge now is actual and no longer metaphoric: whole shorelines swept away and cities and farmland transformed into lakes . . .

Still, there's a certain "wait-and-see" attitude in the folk who hold present power (not to mention the corporate lobbyists and fossil fuel producers), as if the evil that we cannot see is one we need not fear. I can't shake the sense that the brinksmanship threats of nuclear war or the Cuban Missile Crisis seemed a little more pressing, and those behind the wheels of big government today feel they can doze while they drive. Or, perhaps, there's a blind blithe faith in scientific innovation, as if someone in the future will figure out how to reverse-engineer our carbon emissions and lust for reproduction and over-fished oceans and sewage-infested rivers and lakes. A solution deferred is a problem solved, they seem somehow to believe. The legacy we leave our children and our children's children is for them to deal with, because the dead don't care.

This last phrase is a repeated refrain coined by the poet-undertaker Thomas Lynch. In such books as *The Undertaking: Life Studies from the Dismal Trade* (1997), and *Bodies in Motion and at Rest: On Metaphor and Mortality* (2001), he reminds us often that "the dead don't care." Though born and raised in Milford, Michigan, Lynch is Irish Catholic, and one of his masters is, it almost goes without saying, William Butler Yeats. In his essays and in person (for I have visited him in the funeral home operated by his family) he demonstrates the obverse of his four-word pronouncement; the dead may have no feelings but the quick care a great deal. He is compassion itself for those who endure the loss of their loved ones and embark on burial procedures, soliciting his help. And it seems to me, as I grow older, that those of us who may die soon must care as much if not more about the future of the planet as do those who will inhabit it when we—the elders—are dust.

Which brings me to my daughters again, and to their daughters in turn. Some time ago, at her younger sister's first birthday party, the then-six-year-old Penelope offered to make and put up a sign instructing the assembled guests how to dispose of their trash. It was a garden party—paper plates and cups, ice cream, cupcakes, and the paraphernalia of celebration: conical hats, balloons, and bottles of juice and hot dogs on the grill. There were two garbage cans. Penny has an artistic nature; she lettered carefully, colorfully, then Scotch-taped a sheet to the cans. This is what she wrote:

CEEP THE
RTH CLYN
RYYOUS
RYDOOS
RYSIYCL

Her school is a progressive one, earnest in its desire to instruct its students how to salvage and preserve the planet. What she was writing, for those readers who might require translation, was: "Keep the Earth Clean. Re-use. Reduce. Recycle." Yet when my wife offered to help the sign maker with spelling, she shook her curly head and, bending to her task again, said: "I prefer best guess."

From this vantage it does seem that climate change is as widespread a concern of young people as were the fears of radiation when we huddled under desks. The "Green New Deal" has captured the imagination of our youthful politicians, and may—though there's entrenched opposition—have some enduring effect. We've been conditioned by the tale of Chicken Little not to shout the sky is falling because it is, when repeated, a cry no one wants to hear. Of all our mythic heroines, Cassandra is the least attractive; we grow tired of hearing the prophet declare that doom and woe are just around the corner: Catastrophe must come. But there was a moment when "a little child shall lead them," and though I don't imagine that our granddaughters—Anna, Penelope, Rosalie, Frederica, Lydia—or the remarkable Ms. Thunberg will be the world's saviors, it may still prove possible that this younger generation will, as in Chicken Little's story, find the sky fails to fall down . . .

One further mention of funeral rites. When my mother-in-law died, at age ninety-five, she was cremated and kept—by her aging husband—in their closet in a box. When he too died, at ninety-five, it devolved upon my wife and me to deal with their remains. They had lived for nearly sixty years in the town of Wellfleet and it was clear to us—Elena took charge of burial arrangements—that the pair should be interred together in the local cemetery. My own parents had been immigrants, with a less settled sense of location, so "diaspora" seemed appropriate, as opposed to a permanent plot. I scattered my mother's ashes from a small plane above the Green Mountains, in that section of Vermont she loved to visit; our father found his resting place in the Long Island Sound.

But this Cape Cod village was my in-laws' chosen home. Pleasant Hill Cemetery is a peaceful site, with grass-filled alleys and trees and funeral markers dating back to the eighteenth century. Men on tractors mow the lawn and gather fallen branches; at the far reaches of the sloping hill, backhoes dig new plots. There are "Cemetery Rules and Regulations." Here are a few:

1. Lots shall not be used for any other purpose than for the burial of the human dead.
2. Any decorations, artificial flowers and perpetual live flame candles which are inconsistent with the proper keeping of the grounds will not be allowed.
3. No fences of any kind will be permitted.
4. A monument shall not exceed two-thirds of the plot width in length, one foot width and a maximum height of 38"
5. A permanent vault of some type must be used. No wooden boxes will be permitted.
6. Two interments (vault with casket) in one grave will not be allowed, except in the case of a parent and infant child.

There are twenty-nine such rules and regulations, but it's a "laid-back" locale, a rural retreat with moss-encrusted headstones and American flags aflutter in the offshore wind. There are few elaborate monuments or jars of plastic flowers; there's only the sound of distant cars and the caw of gulls. My wife and I are taxpayers in Wellfleet, having inherited her family's house. One spring afternoon we went to the Town Hall to check if there was available space for her parents and then asked to purchase a lot.

The town clerk and treasurer knew Elena, slightly, and did recognize her name. Her father was much honored by the "locals," since he'd given concerts in Wellfleet, and brought young cellists to town. Too, he loved his sailboats, loved to sail, and for decades kept a mooring at the dock.

The clerk unfolded a map. "Bernie was famous," she said. "Let's bury him next to the other famous guy—Edmund Wilson. There's some room."

My wife said, "Thanks. It isn't necessary." Her father and the eminent critic had known each other a little, perhaps, but weren't close—and it seemed needless to insist on their proximity below ground.

"OK." The clerk perused the cemetery map, frowning a little and sucking her pen nib. Then she visibly brightened and pointed to a section of the grid. "We can put him—both of them—next to the other Jew. How's that?"

Now there her parents lie—and someday their daughter and son-in-law will too—on a tree-shaded slope with low shrubs and shells and stones in the grass. "Next to the other Jew..." I doubt it matters much to them, however, since "the dead don't care."

Again, from "A Prayer for the Daughters":

> The fellow who so famously killed King Laius at a crossroads got to sleep with Mummy as reward. It didn't turn out all that well for Oedipus, of course, but for some years in Thebes he was very much respected and obeyed...Yet his counterpart, Electra, had a harder time

of it; she and her brother Orestes did away with their mother and wicked stepfather in order to revenge dear Dad, not to share his bed. And then there were all those Furies to contend with, all that atoning to do . . .

Freud writes of this, it seems to me, with a kind of clear-eyed confusion: The Electra complex has been less celebrated in our culture than the Oedipus. The "mother's son" has been widely assessed, the "father's daughter" less so. Might this not be the case, perhaps, because Dr. Freud and his wife had six children, of whom the famous one is Anna, who carried on as guardian of his work? So the parable becomes instead the story of Lot with his salt daughters or Lear and Cordelia alone in the cell, chatting cheerfully, playing party games and holding each other: God's spies.

I'm not being fair here, obviously, and write this tongue-in-cheek. I've donned the robes of old Mr. Curmudgeon to make an obvious point: The parent-child relationship has altered over time. Altered also with the teller's vantage, and mine should be located so that the reader may triangulate perspective—taking a reading, as it were, on the writer's point of view. My own is that of a father who, when young, did what he could to alienate the affections of other men's daughters from their own fathers and must school himself to like it now while others do the same.

I thought long and hard about marriage—what it would mean in general terms and which specific woman I would ask to be my wife. Once married, I thought with some degree of focus on what it would entail to become and be a father. But I gave scarcely any thought to the matter of being or becoming a grandfather; that was, I told myself, something old people dealt with and not a pressing concern. It was in the cards, perhaps, but not in the hand I was playing.

When I remembered my grandparents—three of whom had been alive for much of my own childhood—it was from a distance. They had been present absences to whom I was polite. Our interactions were formal and respectful, in part perhaps because of the "old world" nature of their expectations and their own nineteenth-century childhoods, in part because they seemed to me like creatures from another planet: plump, speaking heavily accented English, smoking cigars, drinking schnapps.

But now that I'm a grandfather—five times over, with five granddaughters—I ask myself if those young girls consider me also a stranger, not in terms of name or face recognition but in terms of the way I behave. I don't understand the rules of their games or the lyrics of the songs they sing; I'm incompetent at the technologies with which they're already at ease. I feel much closer to my grandparents now than was the case when they were alive, and the bemused inattention with which these children tolerate my eccentricities feels all too familiar. They run where I walk; they dance with agile abandon while I twirl in stately measure on the kitchen floor.

Frederica, now ten, delights in "teaching" me ballet; she goes to dance class and comes back determined to demonstrate the details of an arabesque or jeté. I huff and puff and raise my arms above my head and bend and glide, or try to, as she instructs me, and my evidenced incompetence elicits gales of laughter. At eighty, I pretend to youth in a way my own grandparents didn't, or couldn't, and it pleases me to be the buffoon-like butt of the joke. But sometimes I remember what it felt like to watch my parents and grandparents dance on those few formal occasions they did so, and a sidelong glance in the mirror reveals my father's face.

He died at ninety-eight. Two years before his actual demise he took a fall and was hospitalized. Fearing this would be our farewell visit, I flew east. When I entered the hospital room, he raised his white head and opened his eyes and said to me, "I am not dying yet. But I am more ready for death than for life."

Those sentences have stayed with me. I wonder at what moment and in how near or distant a future I will say the same. "I am more ready for life than for death" is the way I'd at present rephrase it, because there's been such comfort in what Yeats called "the country of the young." A principal delight, these years, is quite precisely the one I did not plan for or envision: being an old person who watches his children's children grow. This is a commonplace feeling—almost everyone I know responds in the same way to our newfound circumstance—but it does not diminish the joy. To have grandchildren and to see them growing is, purely and simply, a gift.

One of the ways a grandparent may imagine immortality posits the survival of future generations; it's how we tell ourselves an afterlife exists. To live on in recollection is to continue to breathe. Those of us who have no faith in spirit-life beyond bodily existence can nonetheless believe we may be remembered, and fondly, by those who carry on. Our children are in this regard less than faithful stewards, of how "we may be remembered"; they're too involved in their own lives to pay sustained attention to their immediate elders. It hurts, at times, to feel so side-lined and irrelevant, but it's in the natural order of things and useless to complain. Instead, I dream of kinfolk reading about my life at some point in the future and finding in these lines a marker of their vanished past. The family album or old home revisited or story recounted or shadow-face in the mirror is in this sense an index not so much of what is transient as of immortality: tricked time.

Some time ago (and before the pandemic's injunction against public gatherings) my wife and I attended a memorial service for a friend who died at seventy. He had been ill but brave and still at work near what now seems an "early" death. There were many luminaries in the hall: editors and authors, mostly from Manhattan, with a sprinkling of figures from southern Vermont, where he'd had his second home. The service took place in the CUNY Graduate Center Foundation, an imposing Fifth Avenue building that once had been the high-end clothing store B. Altman's. Where they'd sold jewelry and gowns and gloves and suitcases we mourners took our seats.

A student string quartet played J. S. Bach, then Samuel Barber's "Adagio for Strings." A wall-sized photograph of the man we'd come to celebrate, sitting cross-legged in his book-lined study, smiled down at us from the stage. A publisher (Jonathan Galassi) was the MC; a Vermont neighbor (Jamaica Kincaid) spoke of his devotion to miniature golf; a biographer (Stacey

Schiff) spoke of his generous tutelage in their shared profession. I've kept his name (James Atlas) out of these paragraphs until this sentence, because the subject of the testimonials was his life as a family man. And privacy not reputation was the occasion's text.

His two children and his elder brother spoke, and the portrait that emerged by ceremony's end was of a devoted husband, father, and grandfather. Atlas was—I don't mean this in the pejorative sense, though that too was part of the package—a "careerist"; he was indefatigable as biographer, editor, journalist, and publisher. His first book, a biography of Delmore Schwartz, came out some forty years before his last, *The Shadow in the Garden: A Biographer's Tale* (2017). That book (and its small sequel, a remembrance of time spent with Philip Roth) celebrated the persistence and mourned the evanescence of the writer's trade. My signed copy of "a biographer's tale" has, as part of its inscription, "congratulations to us for surviving the writing life." His cramped handwriting remains on the page, but the man himself is gone, as are his aspirations; the book may have a lasting shelf life, but its author failed to survive.

What remains are memories: the son reporting on the way the father knew the names of all his puppets, the brother recalling his backhand in tennis, the daughter reading passages of her dear parent's prose. It's the family not the professional man that emerged from this public event, and that is as it should be. As the testimonials ended, and we filed out for wine and canapés, I found myself gauging the size of the crowd and the number of recognizable faces, and then I felt embarrassed because "the dead don't care."

Here's the end of "A Prayer for the Daughters":

> For years we were inseparable as a quartet, going everywhere together and sharing one roof. Now time and the river have done their slow work, and we're together only rarely and on prearranged occasions. This is as it should be. But always, still, as soon as possible—and it delights their parents always—the two of them go off together and, from behind their shared closed door, the sound of laughter comes. . . .
>
> What I pray now for my daughters is that they will have children whose fathers admire them as much as I do mine. And what I pray for those children is that their mothers prove as splendid a mother as is and has been their own. I want them safe. I want them healthy, not ill or at risk. I want them protected from want. I mean them to know what they mean.

A minority opinion. Almost everyone I know by now has fallen under the spell of their pasts and participated in, if not ancestor worship, a hunt for origin-stories. It's fashionable to engage in such tracking, like truffle-hounds snouting for roots. Whether through Ancestry.com or 23 and Me or some other such genealogy site, there's a hydra-headed industry that promises to deliver the verdict on who you are and your ancestors were by virtue of your sampled DNA. This backward-facing analysis has its defenders as well as debunkers, but the scientific basis of such scrutiny is almost an irrelevance: The widespread yearning for authenticated origins has grown all-pervasive now. We each descend from Eve and Adam, yes, but inheritance gets scrambled and the line of descent needs untangling. Identity gets ratified by whether your great-great-grandmother came from the Gobi Desert or sub-Saharan Africa or the Andes or the Ural Mountains, and whether great-great granddad wielded a spear or a plow. If you're Ashkenazi or Sephardim or 1/128th Lakota, you have a specific heritage to honor and enact; if your father's mother's father's mother wore a homespun shawl or wool serape or silk scarf with a spun-gold fringe, you come from a tradition that's wrapped around your neck.

I find all this peculiar. And I understand I've not been fair in the describing, not paid sufficient honor to the idea of identity as an inherited thing. Indeed, a good proportion of this inquiry deals with what went before—and how, when looking in the mirror, I see my father's face. But the desire to know one's origin-story seems far less compelling than the desire to know where it leads, and my imagination is much more fully engaged by future generations than by the vanishing past.

My own ancestry, as far as I can trace it, begins in Venice in the late fifteen hundreds. In the fifteenth century there were Delbancos in Padua, but who they were before they became—as the name suggests—bankers (moneylenders) is not for me to know. I am familiar with the family name before it was transliterated into Italian, and have read the story of Anselmo del Banco, who was very rich. He had a home on the Grand Canal, a building that John Ruskin, in his book on Venice, called "a great stone pile."

Some years ago, on a visit to that city, my wife and I tracked the palazzo down. From the opposite bank of the Grand Canal

I gazed at it mournfully, imagining that I might be the heir of such a lasting legacy and looking down from—instead of looking up at—the high arched windows of the fourth floor. Theatrical, I sighed. "How are the mighty fallen."

Elena applied a much-needed corrective. "They had no heat."

"But furs. They would have worn furs."

"They had no plumbing," she said.

"Servants would have carried out the slops."

"Darling, they would have had bad teeth and little fresh water to wash with. They'd die young and stink."

The fantasy collapsed. My gondolier became thin air, my serving wench a fat toothless hag. The three-hundred ducats that Anselmo del Banco is reported to have offered to the poor in St. Mark's Square each Christmas are no longer mine to squander or, out of charity, spend. The Grand Canal has sewage and oil slicks and the risk of devastating flooding and too many tour boats to count.

"You are old, Father William," the young man said,
"And your hair has become very white;
And yet you incessantly stand on your head—
Do you think, at your age, it is right?"

These lines from Lewis Carroll—recited by Alice in Wonderland—may stand as a template for continuity in change. Father William's antics—standing on his head, doing a somersault at the door, eating a goose, bones and all, then balancing an eel on his nose—are scarcely the gestures of an elder, and no doubt the feats that the poem describes are performed by a man in life's prime. They're both remarkable and silly, both impressive and absurd. I often feel, these early mornings at my desk, that I'm engaged in equivalent antics: contorting a phrase and revising a line till the blank page turns black. There are no acrobatics involved, but the young man's question—"Do you think, at your age, it is right?"—has increasing urgency. Why bother, I ask myself, why should I care, or anybody elsewhere care, that the daily quota has been filled, the daily ablution performed?

It's largely a function of habit, of procedure established so far in the past that youth and middle age required it; now old age requires it too. In terms of religious belief I'm not and never have been credulous. Yet the "things of this world" have an afterlife that I don't believe our body does—or the part of the body that once was called "soul." Since I have no faith in a world beyond our present one, the places and people that live on in recollection are what constitute eternity until both breath and memory are gone.

Some time ago, on the local radio, I heard a lobsterman describe his daily excursion off the shores of Martha's Vineyard: his daily retrieval of what's been entrapped in a pot. He had become too old, he said, to be serious about it, too weak to bait and set more than one pot per trip, and in a small boat. He didn't need the money and had other sources of food. He was down, he declared, to an eighteen-footer with a single outboard motor, but never knew what would come up when he hauled, and it was always exciting though soon he'd have to quit . . .

I knew him in my "salad days," when he owned a fish market in Menemsha for which I, in summertime, worked. His name was Everett Poole; his father's name was Donald; his son is

Donald too. He would die at ninety-one, in February 2022, but then he was gruff and efficient and filleted fish at lightning speed, a pipe or unlit cigar clamped between his teeth, a cap on his bald head. That he continued lobstering, as did generations of Pooles before, meant he was as cussed and hardy as had been his ancestors, and mid-life is an empty term for those who've long survived it.

Or, perhaps, the word should be "outlasted" it, since the voice on WCAI echoed the voice I hear in my mind's ear: "Clean that bass, goddamit; don't let them guts slop all over the floor!" Or, incredulous, "That swordfish weighs only two-hundred pounds; you need help in lifting it?" Or how he cradled the telephone between his right shoulder and chin, saying, "Poole's Fish Market," to a call-in customer, a pencil stub in his right hand, and a yellow sheet on which he scribbled down an order for lobster or flounder or clams . . .

In old or middle age we find ourselves hearing such voices and seeing such scenes and repeating such lines often. It's the way the past revisits us and we, remembering, retrieve it. Proust's madeleine in this regard is a stand-in for the tastes and sounds and sights and smells that trigger our sense-memory. When hearing my old boss-friend's gravelly growl on the radio I was transported to the time in the mid-1960s when I too chomped on an unlit cigar and wore knee-high rubber boots and a green reeking long-sleeved shirt with the name Poole's stitched in red above the pocket.

The clatter and clank of boats at the dock, the fog horn bleating at the harbor's mouth, the sound of a car's engine idling while the girl with a ponytail hurries in for the order her mother placed the night before, which must be retrieved from the cooler: All these return to me as if there were no interval between the then and now. Everett Poole went out in his lobster boat each morning, weather permitting; I do much the same.

The categories "fisherman" and "writer" bear no closer scrutiny than do "horse" and "shoe." But there's one additional equivalence that argues similarity: the catching of fish and the selling of fish are separate occupations. The first can be done by an amateur, the second, a licensed practitioner, and though both belong to the "business" (of fishing or, by analogy, writing) they feel in essence distinct. Our professional lives blur such distinctions and make the private public, but the old man hauling lobsters or finishing a paragraph does so for the pure pleasure of the challenge and to examine what's caught in the net. The middle years, that betwixt and between, have vanished into air.

March 2, 2023, was the forty-ninth anniversary of my mother's death. She passed away at sixty-one, quietly, of a brain tumor. My pregnant wife and I spent the last weeks of the patient's life in the family house in Larchmont, and often at her side in the bedroom where she lay. But we had to leave and travel north on what turned out to be her final morning. I remember driving through winter weather and after five hours reaching our door and opening it to hear the telephone ring.

The call brought the news of her death. This was long before the era of the cell phone, and we'd been out of reach. Although not unexpected, and although I had been well prepared, it nevertheless seemed telling that the dying woman would expire the very morning we left. We did our necessary business, then turned around and drove back south through the snow. At the time I put the crisscrossing misadventure down to a form of coincidence, and the irony of unavoidable commitment elsewhere. My bereavement was not based on proximity or absence on the instant of my mother's demise—if we sat at the bedside or not. We buried her next day.

Then, years later (on March 25, 2006), my mother-in-law died—also in her own home and bed, though in this instance of old age. We'd traveled far to reach her side—an airplane flight, a rental car, a two-hour drive—and my wife was present when she took her final breath. The hospice worker said to Elena, in effect: "Your mother loved you so much she wanted you with her at the end; she waited for you to get here . . ."

And we were consoled. Soon my sister-in-law arrived at the house, too late to see her parent but in time to view the corpse. The same hospice worker took her hand, saying, "Your mother loved you so much she didn't want you to see her die." There's a bromide, in effect, for every circumstance and every form of parting, and I applaud the hospice worker for having comfort at the ready. The dying woman either did or did not want the comfort of her daughters' presence, or perhaps she was indifferent and valued both alike.

But the absolute opposition of those two sentences—*She loved you so much she waited for you to arrive* and *She loved you so much she didn't want you to witness her death*—was startling, and the double-edged or coded discourse I've been describing here. What comforts *A* is useless to *B;* what *C* and *D* receive by way of consolation is not, as a sentence, the same.

Now, for *Still Life at Eighty*, I have composed many thousands of words about my present circumstance. It's not, as any reader who has reached this point will recognize, a standard memoir or full-fledged autobiography. Indeed, the final entry of *Curiouser and Curiouser* (2017) is the tripartite "Towards an Autobiography," and there the interested reader can find details and the data of this so-far life.

Any such document must be provisional. An epitaph or—more extensively—an obituary is the only authoritative summary of life lived. And it too is provisional. Remembrance changes; reputations change. So even this text does not contain, I hope, the final word, and this installment of the whole should be read as a kind of reprise.

Certain themes recur. It's clear, or so I hope, that art and family and travel have mattered much to me; it's clear as well that houses and colleagues and incremental age and marital devotion are matters that absorb me, and have done for years. Therefore, what I've tried to do is link the personal and public, the specific and the general, in ways that reflect upon and refract each other; the most recent of these efforts is not, I trust, the last.

"Count no man happy till you know his end," as the Greeks aver. And though I cannot of course recount my own end, at this stage I call myself happy; these entries attest to an at-least-provisional contentment. That which once seemed urgent now feels evanescent; *this* ambition and *that* disappointment fade. What restlessness and sorrow have been here recorded belong to a fleeting feeling of insufficient accomplishment, as though there were always more laurels to wear and better wine to drink.

The Romantics called it "divine discontent," and my grandmother used to call it "being spoiled."

Both, I think, are true. We have a whole host of sayings to describe this (perhaps peculiarly Western) condition: The glass is half full or half empty, the doughnut shows a ring of pastry or a central hole. "What's sauce for the goose is sauce for the gander" is another way of saying that true distinctions can be difficult to draw; the cooked goose and the living one belong to the same species. So do the female and male or the nonbinary "they." Whether we're discussing a glass, a doughnut, or a goose it's possible to view them in separate ways, and when those views are oppositional a kind of standoff ensues.

I'm conflating here, again, large conflicts such as border wars between Iran and Iraq or Russia and Ukraine with the small-scale opposition of two emotional world views, but it seems fair to notice that the two interpretations are hip-joined if disjunct. "She loved you so much she waited for you to arrive" and "She loved you so much she didn't want you to witness her death" capture the same final scene.

This ability to hold two opposing ideas in one mind at the same time is—as many have observed—the mark of a first-rate intelligence. F. Scott Fitzgerald is reputed to have coined that fine phrase, but there are many others who propose the same. There's a book by John Donatich called *Ambivalence: A Love Story* (2005) with its subtitle "Portrait of a Marriage." This in turn refers to *Portrait of a Marriage* (1973) by Nigel Nicolson: a son's fond revelatory remembrance of his parents' complicated union—his parents being the diplomat Harold Nicolson and Vita Sackville-West (who was, among other things, the lover of

Virginia Woolf and the subject of that 1928 biographical extravaganza, *Orlando*). Ambivalence is everywhere attendant on decision making, and those to whom the emotion is foreign seem in some sense limited. There's no assertion so absolute that it doesn't have a contrary assertion, unless perhaps you choose to question the absolute authority of the preceding phrase.

Does "high and dry" mean safe or stranded? Is it a circumstance to wish for or condition to avoid? Is "downhill from here" a way of saying things will get easier or harder? Or consider the phrase "cut and trim." Does it suggest a tailor's expertise, a logger or lumberjack's practice, a readiness to compromise? Might it suggest instead a failure of conviction and a loss of nerve? Is it a habit to foster or change? Is the person who cuts and trims someone to blame or to praise?

The word "nice" comes from the Anglo-Saxon *nysse,* meaning "not to know." This construct was in opposition to the term *wysse,* the "wisdom" of a wise person. Thus the "nice" distinction drawn by a courtier in Shakespeare is demonstrably a stupid one, and it took centuries before the term became a compliment. Now "nice" is once again subject to intonation; it can either be an insult or a term of praise.

By accentuating these oppositions, I've attempted to highlight the doubled perception, which seems a crucial marker of self-awareness in the post-Freudian individual. There's no such thing as ambivalence in allegory—where a figure represents one attitude, one attitude alone. In most early texts (think of *Everyman* or *Pilgrim's Progress*) we know at once who will behave in what way. The figures are allegorical, representative, and they do not change. Before the age of the Enlightenment, and then the inward-facing focus of the Romantics, white was white, black black.

Now the complex shaded figure is the one who claims attention. We're not wholly brave or cowardly but a mixture of the two; we're neither entirely generous nor miserly but go back and forth between opposing impulses; we're smart or stupid by turn. It's the tension and the friction between those seeming contradictions that generate dimension, where a character on the page or stage has some of the complexity of life. As William Faulkner put it in his Nobel Prize address (1950), the writer should deal with "the problems of the human heart in conflict with itself which alone can make good writing because only that is worth writing about, worth the agony and the sweat." Ambivalence or double-sidedness is built into the construct of a character, and any persuasive rendition of a knight in shining armor must also have a stain upon the gleaming metal: Achilles has his heel.

One further name to add to this litany of loss. Each week brings the name of a writer who dies, and in January 2023 it was Russell Banks. In honor of "ambivalence or double-sidedness," I want to celebrate his memory, though there's no ambivalence here. I spent time with him in Saratoga Springs, Miami, Ann Arbor, Keene, Manhattan, Albany, and elsewhere. At the Association of Writers & Writing Programs in Albany, long years ago, we shared a panel. The topic was something predictable like "Who is Our Audience" or "Whither Fiction," and when Banks rose to speak he was eloquence itself.

The little painter

Standing with my father, Kurt Delbanco, in front of a Willem de Kooning oil, 1994. Photo by Elena Delbanco.

The portrait of Frances Lehmann Bernstein, by Max Liebermann, 1926

Publicity photo for *Consider Sappho Burning*, 1969. Photo by Peter Simon.

With John Gardner, 1977. Photo by Joel Gardner.

With Max Eastman, 1967, in Martha's Vineyard.
Photo by Peter Simon.

Elena with Grace Paley at the house in Ann Arbor, 2007

At the PEN/Faulkner Award Ceremony in Washington, DC.
Rear row: Nicholas, Grace Paley, Russell Banks, Molly Gloss,
E. L. Doctorow; *front row*: Ellen Douglas, Lynne Sharon Schwartz,
and Josephine Jacobsen, 1989.

At the PEN/Malamud Award Ceremony in Washington, DC.
Rear row: Nicholas, Janna Malamud, Emily Maxwell; *front row*:
Ann Malamud, Stuart Dybek, and William Maxwell, 1995.

With Richard Elman and William Kennedy in Vermont, 1981

Andrea and Francesca in New York, 2023

Our five granddaughters, 2022. *Left to right*: Frederica Stoller, Anna Shalom, Rosalie Shalom, Lydia Stoller, and Penelope Stoller.

The Ekoi mask

The Biedermeier desk

The Countess of Stanlein
ex-Paganini Stradivarius
violoncello case

Nicholas and Elena: "Still Life at Eighty"
in the Wellfleet garden, 2022

The audience was large—mostly writers, mostly young. Russ delivered an impassioned diatribe about the writer's life, saying that as an author he was necessarily a rebel, a contrarian, beholden to no one and riding solo through the badlands of society, his six-gun at the ready and his targets pride and pomp. As a tax-paying citizen, he tried to stay within the law; as an artist, never. We were outlaws, first to last. There was huge agreement in the audience, a standing ovation. But as he sat while hundreds stood applauding, he turned to me and said, "Of course, I'm also a tenured professor at Princeton." Both were true.

A sufficient change in quantity brings qualitative change. There's a difference, as Karl Marx observed, in a fight between two men and a war with two million on either side; the quantity of the combatants brings a qualitative difference to the fray. If one object weighs an ounce and another weighs a ton they may be similar in contour but unalike in scale. To write at eighty of a life gone by is not the same as to do so at eighteen or forty-eight. To ignore such distinctions is—to use a cognate word and substitute noun for verb—a form of ignorance. Adjacent to ignorance is that additional term, intolerance.

Think of the word "conventional." As a descriptor nowadays it's come to mean "uninteresting" or "commonplace" or "dull." But "conventional wisdom" means something quite different, and the term is generally approbatory; it means an agreed-on set of standards for behavior. Similarly, the word "original" has several shades of meaning; the tone of voice with which one says, "He's an original," means either that the character in question is one of a kind or a fool.

Ambivalence resides these days in the anxious response to a sneeze or a cough. (I first felt this anxiety at the start of the pandemic, and three years later it still seems to be the case.) We're told to watch such symptoms closely, and if there's a sore throat or ache and pain in the chest, if there's fever or a headache—*voilà,* pussycat.

Yet one can have such symptoms without the coronavirus, and at the end of winter there are allergies abounding, as well as RSV and standard-issue colds and stomach flus. It's hard to know, in short, how much to worry if your own throat tickles or the person next to you displays a runny nose. My wife's chest feels heavy, congested, and I remind her that childhood bouts of asthma have inclined her to bronchitis. Which we both pray is true.

In the Middle Ages, the "scourge of God" was thought to be instructive: a visitation of the plague meant sinners were being punished. The example of such suffering could help engender penance; the holy were hale, the unholy unclean. It was easy enough in theory—though no doubt hard in practice—to ascribe one's pain and misery to the judgment of an all-seeing god, whose verdict often was harsh. But today we're inclined to blame the Chinese or, perhaps, the Russians, in those lands beyond the pale from which corruption comes. And there's a "germ" of truth in the problem posed by interconnectedness as opposed to isolation; in our present world the ability of humankind to traverse great distances quickly is part of the problem and not the solution. No outbreak can be isolated now.

A related case, perhaps, is that of global war. You could not mount or enact a Crusade without long arduous travel and, in the end, hand-to-hand combat. But an assault on the World Trade Center could be masterminded and controlled by a man in a cave a world away, who had nothing tactile to do with the explosion produced.

This interconnectedness changes the rules of engagement; what happens ten thousand miles distant comes to our doorstep too. A pandemic can arise much more swiftly and expansively in the age of airplane travel than when travel required a camel, horse, or ship. All this by way of saying that what Blake called "the invisible worm," is beyond our grasp or reach to contain; the virus arrived from seeming-nowhere. Whether it originated in a laboratory or a live market in Wuhan or a bat-cave in the Ural mountains, or some other scenario cooked up by conspiracy theorists is moot; from nowhere it has grown everywhere rampant and will not soon subside. To live with this new knowledge is to live in fear.

Als ob is German for "as if," and it first found important expression in the work of Immanuel Kant. Then the scholar Hans Vaihinger elaborated on the phrase in his *Philosophie des Als Ob* (*Philosophy of As If*, 1911) in which he propounded the notion that certain ideas cannot be confirmed but must be acknowledged as if their veridicality were proved. Now those of us who sneeze and cough should behave *als ob* we are infected by a virus that might plausibly prove fatal. And the repeated injunctions of the medical professionals—"Wear a mask, Don't touch your face, Avoid gatherings of more than ten people"—have had a kind of cumulative effect; the pattern of our daily round is modified and by new patterns replaced.

The Journal of the Plague Year, written by Daniel Defoe in 1722, chronicles in fictive terms the outbreak of plague in London in 1655. *Year of Wonders* (2001), by Geraldine Brooks — though written without irony—does much the same. The bubonic plague remains a major event in our collective consciousness, as does the Spanish influenza pandemic of 1918. These fearsome outbreaks did much more than decimate the populations they affected, since to "decimate" is merely to kill one in ten. To take just one further example, *La Peste,* or *The Plague,* the fierce novel by Albert Camus (1947), is a speculative inquiry into what might happen in Algeria in an imagined scenario from the 1940s. The plague breaks out and levels the city of Oran. Camus uses this contagion to study reactive behavior and construct a template for how the human animal behaves.

Although the bulk of these entries deal with "life," they are death-haunted, clearly. At my stage of age the obituary page is the one I turn to before News or Entertainment or Sports, and not a week goes by without an announcement of loss. At dinner parties, the talk includes a description of funerals and memorial services attended, burial arrangements made, the memory of long-gone parents, siblings, friends, or children afflicted and at risk . . .

For those of us who soldier on, and whose long life-span now shortens, this is both predictable and unavoidable; human consciousness entails a sense of the approaching end. I don't imagine a leaf of grass in a soon-to-be-mowed-meadow or a salmon spawning upstream has a similar alertness—or, rather, what it "thinks" of is not the unplanned future and its own extinction. The soldier in a trench or patient in an ICU may well have just such an awareness, but it belongs routinely to those who have grown old. Of that roster of writers I listed when reporting on the Bennington writing workshops, very few remain alive; I care for fewer of the living than the dead.

"I've never seen anything like this before."
"There's never been anything like this before."
"It's not a thing we know how to manage. To deal with."
"Deal with it."

These lines will be repeated. Although invented, such thoughts are everywhere expressed; the dilemma posed by COVID-19 and its ever-mutating strains does feel omnipresent. A handshake with strangers or cheek-kiss with friends now feels fraught with peril, and variant after variant rekindles our concern about close body-contact. The distribution of vaccines and booster shots is at last widespread, but getting a shot is a time-consuming process and there are many who fear it. The new strains of the virus call into question the efficacy of our response to the old. I have no doubt that dystopian novels are being contracted for in quantity, and television shows whose topic is "contagion" will abound. The uncertainty attested to some lines previous has been replaced by certainty: We're here for the long haul.

What's clear beyond contravening is that COVID-19 earned national attention, and the concomitant threat to the economy has shattered our complacency. The open-ended sense of possibility has closed. It seems somehow important to identify the *source* of the contagion, as if the day we know it is the day it goes away. We don't yet know what aftereffects are likely, what "long COVID" and recurrence will consist of or what further trouble develop in the years ahead.

It's our human habit to behave as if the day after tomorrow will resemble this one, and equally our habit—when that expectation fails—to be surprised until we take for granted what had been shocking before. A dead rat in the street or cluster bomb in the plaza still seem extraordinary until become the norm. A heat wave or bleached coral reef are harbingers of doom. Depression is widespread; the suicide rate and mass shootings increase. The mind reels.

Or, rather, it travels in well-worn circles and old familiar paths. It follows the same pattern over and over, a hamster on a wheel inside a cage. It repeats itself and goes around the question and the effects of quarantine, the way a prisoner might dream about escape and open air. Self-imposed or superimposed, it makes no difference, really; we go back and forth and forth and back upon the single track.

The mind reels. The little daily rounds of habit—waking up and making coffee and listening to morning news and sitting at the desk to type—all seem irrelevant, or suspect, soon to change. A friend stopping by to say hello may be the purveyor of death. The grocery store and place of worship and barber shop and restaurant and movie theater and pump at the gas station feel replete with risk in a way that was unthinkable before. Humanity seems bent upon its own extinction, and all the more so since so repeatedly warned. It's just a matter of time, we fear, before coronavirus—or global warming, violence, and terrorism—will afflict us all.

I've never seen anything like this before."

"There's never been anything like this before."

"It's not a thing we know how to manage. To deal with."

"Deal with it."

Last month there were doctors. I saw a dermatologist who scraped and burned a spot on my shoulder, assuring me the subcutaneous cancer would be slow-growing yet lethal if not stopped. This is the third or fourth such procedure I've had; an unbreakable habit of sitting or working outside, and with too little sunscreen, has left me dark-spotted, at risk. There's a scar on my right shin, a scar on my left arm. Each year I get treated and warned.

Also, I saw an ophthalmologist who urged me to schedule an operation for cataracts—first in the left eye, then right. Although I spend many hours a day staring at the small print I read or produce, I've never needed glasses. Yet, my eyesight is a good deal worse than twenty–twenty. One eye is farsighted, the other nearsighted, and the problems tend to cancel each other out. Were I to wear bifocals, they say, I'd see marginally better, but for years I've made my own adjustments: squint and stare. More and more, however, the world grows blurred and, at night, unreadable; the headlights of oncoming cars are Klieg lights, blinding. Now I resemble my parents and grandparents who huddled beneath a reading lamp and, when scrutinizing headlines, used a magnifying glass.

More seriously, I have a heart condition—angina pectoris—and coronary artery disease. There's a scheduled echocardiogram and stress test in four days. My lifelong history of heart trouble—rheumatic fever when a child, a series of implanted stents, a double-bypass operation and aortic valve replacement—makes this procedure less than routine. My chest tightens when I start to walk; on stairs, my breath grows short. Like many other adult males, I eat and drink too much and exercise too little. It's a constant concern if not anxiety, and I tell myself each morning that this is the day I'll take matters in hand and reverse the downhill slide.

But that slide is called the aging process, and I'm an elderly person. The size of my stomach and hunch of my shoulders feel irreversible; the pace of my walk has slowed. What I'll manage on the treadmill will no longer be an athlete's stride, and even at "the top of my game" I wasn't very good. But there was a time I lifted weights and jogged miles each morning; it's all behind me now.

This is standard stuff for those who grow old; the "organ recital" is our anthem if not our habitual song. And it should be kept in context; I've outlived the actuarial tables my parents and grandparents knew. They were in fact a long-lived crew; my father's family died, routinely, in their nineties, my mother's in their eighties, and I have no reason to believe an Appointment in Samarra will be kept this day or week. On the list of diseases and medical conditions a patient must complete when visiting a doctor's office, I check off very few. In the standard parlance of politeness, people say how young I look and compliment my vigor in old age. My older brother is well into his eighties, my younger brother, his seventies, and we're a sturdy bunch.

Why should mortality disturb me now; why not excise the "t" and write about morality instead? Or, perhaps, the nature of those things I'm so reluctant to relinquish? If, as Prospero avers, "Every third thought shall be my grave," what of the other two? Let me think about the life and death of objects, of treasured possessions, *things of this world*: how they outlast their owners, and what divestiture means.

After a thirty-year residence in Ann Arbor, Elena and I retired from the University of Michigan, where we both had worked. There seemed no reason to stay by ourselves in what once had been the family home, and we put it on the market and prepared to leave. As those who've done something similar know, this is a stressful project and process. We "downsized."

There were three categories of objects to deal with: *junk, still serviceable, treasured*. The first contained the usual detritus of long occupancy: frayed dish towels, threadbare rugs, broken coffee pots and chipped drinking glasses and cracked pottery. There were several thousand books to donate to the library or pulp. There were old suitcases and blankets to offer to the homeless, old tables and chairs to put out on the street, old clothes to take to Goodwill. Outmoded television sets and tape recorders and portable radios could be recycled at the Transfer Station, a closely supervised facility that used to be called the Town Dump.

In an autumnal frenzy of spring cleaning, we gave away or jettisoned carloads and truckloads of objects, emptying shelves and closets from the four floors of the house. Three-legged chairs and broken umbrellas and summer-camp memorabilia and high-school yearbooks and the hedge trimmer and lawnmower I'd planned to repair all were consigned to the trash. A bed and standing goosenecked lamp and bureau with a missing drawer pull were given to a friend with a suddenly failed marriage who needed to furnish a new place. Habitat for Humanity collected old bunk beds and stools. Rakes with splayed prongs and spades with no handles and a warped ping-pong table with no net and ornamental bottles without bottle caps and cans of old paint "bit the dust."

That phrase bemused me; it conveyed a fallen figure—hero or bum—face down in the dirt. But biting the dust is not quite the same as "biting the bullet," and a trace of satisfaction accompanied the pain. We felt virtuous, pared down. I mourned the books, but kept those that mattered most to me, or that I planned still to read. Faded shirts and tattered coats could cause a pang of nostalgia but would be replaced. Once embarked upon, the process was a cleansing one, and Elena and I pursued it without regret. The category "junk" was simple to deal with and, if anything, our shared reaction was one of relief.

"Still serviceable" proved harder. This sofa and that leather chair had lost their sheen a little, maybe, but retained the imprint of years, sometimes decades, of glad use. This painting and that photograph were without commercial value, but I still paused to study them while walking up or down stairs. Just because there was no open floor seemed less than a good reason to sell that

Navajo rug or kilim carpet; why couldn't or shouldn't we roll them up and store them against further use? We have children and grandchildren, after all, and surely someone sometime in the future would welcome this old hunting horn or that signed baseball or the woven basket I purchased for three dollars in 1968. The desk I sat at meant nothing to others, nor did the pillows we slept on, but that didn't mean—or did it?—they should be discarded. There are storage units available for rental, and one doesn't have to use a thing to retain it. Why not box it up and label it against a rainy day?

This kind of triage is common, and householders engage in it often. "We need a new stove, a new set of curtains, a new car" is the sort of statement that doesn't always signal need; in an economy of planned obsolescence, the replacement of objects is almost routine. Consumers buy new clothes not because the old can no longer be worn but because the fashions change. In used furniture stores or antique shops all across the country your grandmother's tea set is displayed for sale; as are her antimacassars and lamps. That a pot outlives its function for *A* does not mean it's useless for *B*.

A secondary meaning of a transfer station suggests that new owners may profit from objects that have been replaced. The thrift shop and treasure mart are ubiquitous, or nearly, and recycling has become standard practice. This year's detritus is next year's collectible, so "still serviceable" is an elastic category and at least as large as "junk." It can mean "of use to others," once abandoned. Whether stored in an archive or sold to a collector or bargained for on E-Bay or given away to a neighbor or donated to charity, the afterlife of this kind of object can be a lengthy one.

"Treasured" is the problematic category of the three: "things of this world" that have more than mere monetary value. Whether the worth be extrinsic or intrinsic, a treasured object has meaning to those who possess it, a meaning not easy to gauge. The Rembrandt self-portrait that hung on a family's living room wall for generations is in this sense no more important than a sprung-limbed Teddy Bear clutched by a child, or a security blanket stained by nighttime sweat. One might be sold for millions of dollars, the other consigned to the attic, and the third to trash. But each of them is numinous with embedded memory, and all such possessions are hard to relinquish.

Let me examine a trio of "treasures"—three things we retain:

I own a doubled Ekoi mask, a Janus-faced structure with two stylized and similar visages: one dark brown, one pale. They face in opposite directions, yet share a single neck. The age of this African object is hard to determine: less than two hundred and more than eighty years old. The heads have black-painted lines on their full cheeks. Each of the faces is life-sized, or just a touch larger, and when you add the conical hat that covers the opposing profiles the height of the whole is seventeen inches, the width fifteen.

The large wooden visage is covered with skin. As a child I studied the puckering parchment-like surface and was sure it was flayed human flesh. Instead, it's antelope skin. When the mask was first carved out of soft local wood, animal hide was stretched across it, then colored with pigment from bark and leaves. This holds true of the covering skullcap as well, though some fur has remained on the hat.

Both mouths are open and display teeth made of carved bamboo. One set of eyes is closed, one open, signifying death and life. The neck is arched and doubly wide so that the two-faced visage can surround a human head. There are holes at the base of the open neck, through which raffia would have been strung, and the dancer who wore this doubled headdress would be covered, not revealed.

In terms of authenticity, the mask is the real thing. The great distinction, for experts, has to do with intentionality; if the object was created for use and ritual observance, it's "real," but if intended for sale (in airport and tourist shops, or on the street), it's merely merchandise. This piece belongs to the former category, and it will go—when I no longer look at it—either to a museum or, should they request it, a child. The mask came to me from my father, who collected tribal art—as had his mother, earlier. She started to do so in Hamburg, in the early twentieth century, when such artifacts were first being noticed and prized. Picasso and others in Paris fell under the sway of African masks, and they have important value now.

This one comes from southeast Nigeria or, perhaps, the western Cameroons; the term "Ekoi" describes the several tribes who spoke a shared language in the area of Ejagham. When I wrote, above, that the object's age is indeterminate, it's because I know my father owned it as long ago and far away as London, which we left for America in the 1940s. Very few wood-and-skin constructions survive for an extended time before harsh climate takes its toll, and it's therefore safe to assume this prized example of Ekoi craftsmanship made its way to Europe when less than a hundred years old. Without an elaborate process of date testing and analysis, "eighty to two hundred" seems a reasonable guess. The record of provenance states, "Purchased in London from Mr. Ohly, Berkeley Gallery, in 1946." Repatriation was not an issue then; it was simply an object for sale.

Now the mask is a family heirloom, in the sense of long-term ownership, and there are stories attached. I remember Uncle Gustav, for instance, holding the totem aloft and dancing with it in the hall of our house, then somehow managing to get his head inside. I was young—four or five years old—and he might have been tipsy, or hoping to amuse his brother and sister-in-law or trying to frighten my older brother and me.

In the last effort and in my case, he succeeded. The brown wooden Ekoi mask slipped more easily over his head than when he tried to remove it. He nodded and shuffled in circles, and I remember the contrast of his light blue suit and the doubled face above it. At first this seemed amusing, the kind of puckish antic with which, in later life, I learned to identify him. I think I remember we laughed. I think I remember he tottered about, waving his arms and jerking his head up and down. Gustav made high-pitched noises, and only after an interval—five seconds, five minutes, a child's eternity?—did we come to understand that he was saying, "Help!"

What goes down must come up. After a period (my father removing it gently, my mother raising her glass in salutation), the mask slipped free. My uncle emerged red-faced and sweaty, his shock of white hair disarrayed. The smiling and the scowling image—life and death—with its wide-open and close-shuttered eyes, was returned to its place on the shelf. Its expression—expressions—had not changed. But more than seventy years later, when I study its striated face, I see my long-dead uncle wetting his lips inside it and uttering, stuttering, "H-help!"

In a more serious vein and without, I hope, cultural appropriation, I see the Ekoi mask as an emblem of this present effort. It faces both forward and back—one set of eyes closed, one open. The cheeks are full, the teeth carious, the expression both hopeful and grim. It is Janus-faced in the way *Still Life at Eighty* has tried to be throughout, and it was constructed with both craft and art. May the nameless maker of that object rest assured the work is venerated still.

There's a second totemic wooden object, on which the Ekoi mask now stands. This "treasure" is a piece of furniture constructed in the Germany from which my parents later fled: a Biedermeier cabinet-desk. According to Wikipedia, "The Biedermeier period refers to an era in Central Europe between 1815 and 1848, during which the middle class grew in number and arts appealed to common sensibilities. It began with the time of the Congress of Vienna at the end of the Napoleonic Wars and ended with the onset of the European Revolutions of 1848."

Biedermeier is a catchall movement and mode, its artistic hub beginning in Vienna and radiating outwards. The style comprised several art forms: music, painting, architecture, poetry and, in this instance, furniture. My father's middle-class family in Hamburg (though family-proud, and not inclined to think of themselves as having "common sensibilities") fit this particular bill. As this book's illustrations suggest, they had an interest in art. Most of their heavy furniture was fashioned in the

Biedermeier mode, and much of it was lost when they fled Nazi rule. But a container or two of family possessions had been shipped to London, where my uncle Gustav made his home as of the early 1930s and to which my parents repaired.

Some of the furniture was Bauhaus-inspired: sleek chairs and hard-edged tables that came into favor later on. This modernist and pared-back style has retained its currency and flourishes today. But the large Biedermeier desk—more accurate, I think, to describe it as a cabinet—is a time-worn piece and nearly two hundred years old. Like the Janus-faced figure now perched on its flat top, it bears the marks of usage. Small stains and burns and splinters dot the shelves.

The bulky artifact sat in my father's office and then our living room and then his studio all through my youth and young manhood. Its American equivalent would be a roll top desk. I still can see him sitting beside it, the leather-lined writing plank buttressed by a drawer supporting his papers and pens, the photographs of his own father and mother at his left-hand side. Waxed and gleaming, the *burgerliche* object fairly reeks of my dead family, the grandfather I never knew but see in that sepia photo, wearing a white jacket and leaning on a cane.

He stares off into the middle distance, posed yet poised. It had been his desk before, lodged in the import-export firm of which he was the managing director, and to which he gave his name. No doubt it had been stuffed with paper: bills of lading, accounts receivable from suppliers and, for customers, invoices yet to be paid.

The wood is polished maple. Its hue is reddish, edging up to burnt sienna. The pattern of the grain is vivid and pronounced.

There are five drawers, of varying height; the desk is four feet wide. The height of the whole is five-and-a-half feet, the depth, three. The purfling—both vertical and horizontal—is of bright black ebony. The drawers and the doors that open to reveal six separated containers each have a metal keyhole, and the key is lodged for safekeeping in the third drawer down. (I have tried to have it reproduced but not yet found the specialist who could properly copy that key.) The small pull-out containers that are fitted to their cubbyholes each have carved ivory pulls. When the doors are open and the desktop down, it is as though secrets of commerce are being revealed: a prosperity made manifest in those who did business once. The ivory, the patterned oak, the green leather writing surface have looked this way since their creation long ago and an ocean away; there's the after-odor of my mother's cigarettes and her father-in-law's cigars.

Now the drawers act as storage bins and are only rarely opened. One holds tablecloths and cloth napkins and napkin rings we never use; one holds light bulbs and extension cords and batteries. One holds old maps and tax returns and stacked photographs of our friends and children at various stages of age. A fourth contains some graphic art—unframed, with tissue-paper interleaved—that does not hang on the walls. At a future moment, perhaps, I'll extricate the etchings and the lithographs that lie within, and frame or give away or sell them, but that day has not arrived. The "still serviceable" category here coexists with "treasured," for this is a storage unit I've not yet emptied out.

The desk has resale value, but not sufficient to change a bank balance: a few thousand dollars at most. What makes it hard to sell or store is its emblematic nature; I've seen it all my life. When my father offered it to me as a keepsake—he too had been "downsizing"—it was on condition that I pay the costs of transport and the small-scale yet needful carpentry repairs. I did. We were living in Ann Arbor, and the heavy desk had to be shipped. The company that brought the thing to Michigan had been careful, clearly, and wrapped it in layers of plastic and paper and —that curse of the contemporary moment—Styrofoam pellets. Uncrated, it was worked on by a local craftsman who added glue where needed, replaced a section of chipped purfling, and waxed and polished the whole.

When at last it was delivered to our living room and lodged in a safe corner, I felt as though a portion of the past had been restored. And even though the feeling is farfetched, I sense a kind of benison each time I pass the Biedermeier desk. The shapes and shibboleths of the dear dead are clustered near it, smoking and chatting; the ambient air grows thick.

"They're shooting at our battalion," a friend of mine observes, when one of our number (or a person slightly junior, or slightly senior) dies. Obituary notices have long since become required reading for us all, and—to quote again the too-soon-lost James Baldwin—"The royal fellowship of death" inducts new members, year by year.

> Beauty is but a flower
> Which wrinkles will devour;
> Brightness falls from the air;
> Queens have died young and faire;

Dust hath closed Helen's eye.
I am sick, I must die.
Lord, have mercy upon us!

This stanza from Thomas Nashe's "A Litany in Time of Plague" has stayed with me. Nashe lived from 1567 to 1601 and therefore died—by present standards—well before his time. Of an average, and absent the "plague" of war, we live more than twice as long.

In recent years, however, the life expectancy of those who inhabit America has declined. Partly this is because of the suicide and murder rates, partly the epidemic of obesity, partly the number of opiate-related deaths and, lately, COVID-19. The health of the planet has diminished and nears irreversible change. Those of us who now contemplate dust and who watch while brightness falls must try to come to terms with what Nashe described and what his longer-lived contemporary, Shakespeare, called "the fall of a sparrow." Prince Hamlet's stoic acquiescence to the inevitability of death ends with the assertion, "The readiness is all."

My readiness has more to do with death than diminution. I'm not consciously afraid of the loss of consciousness but live in a slow-simmering fear of the loss of bladder or sphincter or mental control. The vegetal condition is one I would hate to endure. Now more and more I tell myself that what I took for granted once has been or is being extinguished. As did Nashe, I study wrinkles upon the "young and faire." Like most of my other sentient friends, I've signed Power of Attorney and Patient

Advocate Forms to insure that DNR—Do Not Resuscitate—is the operative instruction when in my last hospital bed.

But the survival instinct is strong in our species, and hard to counteract or override. A motto for us all is Faulkner's "They endured." Vitality, acuity of intellect, a sensory response to stimuli—a Degas drawing, a Mozart piano concerto, a long-legged blonde on the catwalk or screen—are things to prize and admire. A sunset or glass of good red wine can delight me still.

When, however, I find myself adrift or dreaming (more and more often nowadays), I fear total inattention as the necessary end. A slow withdrawal into inattention is the little daily death. My children and grandchildren whisper and—in my failing hearing—ask me, at the table's head, to "please pass the salt"; they sing songs whose lyrics escape me and strap on masks for Virtual Reality sessions and punch the air. They are quick-fingered where I'm clumsy, adept where I'm adrift. And though I mourn the time when I too was agile, flexible, when late-night celebrations were the rule and not exception, I watch them caper on the lawn with no desire or ability to join their reindeer games. What I feel is unoriginal: not new but new to me.

The third object also is fashioned of wood. It sits in the basement studio of our house in Wellfleet. It has done so since I first saw it there, in the mid-1960s, when I was courting Elena. Then the home belonged to her parents, and the basement was a climate-controlled retreat in which her father practiced and taught. Bernard Greenhouse was a soloist, a founding member of the Bach Aria Group and, importantly, the Beaux Arts Trio. As of

1955, this chamber music ensemble made piano trio literature as consequential to the repertoire as that of string quartets.

I wrote a book titled *The Beaux Arts Trio: A Portrait* in 1985. By then they had been concertizing for fully thirty years and set the bar for achievement in the domain of piano trio performance and discography. I also wrote a book about the two-year-long painstaking repair and restoration of Greenhouse's prized violoncello: *The Countess of Stanlein Restored* (2001). This began as an article for *Harper's* magazine, and was thereafter expanded into a volume with the jaw-cracking subtitle "A History of the Countess of Stanlein ex-Paganini Stradivarius Violoncello of 1707." Having interviewed my father-in-law, I quoted him at length about his much-celebrated instrument, its attributes and provenance. He had carried the cello all over the world and, when he died in 2011, the "Countess" lay in his bed at his side.

That particular piece of wood has a long and storied history, and it too set the standard of excellence in what is admittedly a rarified domain. Though there are several hundred documented examples of violins made by the fabled luthier from Cremona, only a few dozen of his larger wooden instruments remain. The template for the modern violoncello was established by Antonio Stradivari (1644–1737), and "The Countess" (1707) is a prime example of the form. My book-length inquiry into the nature of the object—its proportions and varnish and the method of construction, its structural, aesthetic, and acoustic attributes, its sequence of previous owners—need not be reproduced here. In any case the cello no longer stays under our roof; after Elena's father died, we put "The Countess" up for sale in order to settle the artist's estate.

Too, Bernard Greenhouse had wanted it played. Like any other instrument, it would lose resonance if not performed upon. An oil painting or tapestry may hang on a wall undisturbed for centuries and retain its beauty; an echo chamber made out of wood—no matter how splendid to look at—is intended to be heard.

At the height of his career, Greenhouse became a collector. The Countess of Stanlein was, clearly, the jewel in the crown, but he also owned an eighteenth-century violoncello built by "the Spanish Stradivarius," José Contreras. He amassed examples of the work of French instrument makers, of German and English and American and, finally, Chinese practitioners of the luthier's trade. Most of these were without much value, offered up to his students during lessons and to junior colleagues for practice sessions; they lay out on couches or atop a Steinway piano or in a companionable jumble at the edges of the studio. Indeed, "The Countess" had been copied by a series of luthiers, who studied the proportions of the great original and tried to reproduce it to the millimeter.

So there it stood, for decades, a pearl among white peas . . .

Since such instruments must travel—in cars and trains and planes—they need to be protectively encased. The risks of accidental encounter—being dropped or poked or spilled upon—are real, and cellists routinely pack their instruments away when not in use. Of late there are hard plastic cases, Plexiglas cases, cloth-covered cases built out of pressboard, even cases forged out of aluminum or titanium. The wear and tear of climate change (a performance one night in a hot humid hall, the next day in an arid, air-conditioned one) needs to be accounted for, and a violoncello should fit inside its traveling companion like a hand in glove.

The first case Greenhouse used for his "Strad" came from the brothers Hill. W. E. Hill and Sons is perhaps the most famous company in the business of bowed wooden musical instruments, and has been established in London since 1880. Successive generations of the family plied the luthier's trade. They were violin makers, bow makers, purveyors of the work of others, and historians of the commerce of sales; in their field they have a stature almost equivalent to that of Stradivarius, and it seemed only fitting that "The Countess" should be sequestered in and protected by an artifact from the brothers Hill.

Greenhouse had purchased the instrument in Germany from a private family, the Talbots. The cello had been theirs for generations, and I know the details of his acquisition but am not in fact quite certain how and when he acquired the case. Did he buy it while concertizing in London? Was it provided by the New York dealer, Rembert Wurlitzer, whose shop foreman, Fernando Sacconi, first worked on the violoncello once it crossed the Atlantic? Was it given to him as a kind of promotional gesture by W. E. Hill and Sons, as a way of basking in the reflected glory of the Strad? Since it is in effect impregnable, did it serve as an insurance policy for the priceless object within?

Whatever the origin-story, the case sits today, resplendent, in a reconditioned studio near the sea in Massachusetts. The room itself has been emptied of its dozen instruments and its grand piano and now is filled with books. As with the Biedermeier desk, this object has been repurposed and serves as a reminder—decorative, nonfunctional—of a distant past. Where once it held a violoncello—and bows, and resin, and musical scores—it now contains nothing but air. Of the performer's collection, there remains this single artifact: a sentry standing at attention after the army was demobilized and one by one dispersed.

A cello's front and rear "plates" are fashioned from maple; so is the instrument's scroll. Its "ribs" are spruce, the interior blocks carved from willow, and the fingerboard is ebony. This container too has been sawed out of wood. It has two metal handles with which to lift and carry it, but the case itself is oak, and can best be described as weighty. Empty, the thing weighs twenty-four pounds. It has beveled edges and, like the Biedermeier cabinet's shelves, has interior linings attached, though the fabric is not felt but silk. A small metal plate is affixed to the rear, inscribed with the address of the Hill brothers company. The long "neck" of the instrument and the broad beam of its "belly" have been replicated—exaggerated, even—by the angled outer shape. A middle section of the front-facing plate has been raised to accommodate the cello's fingerboard, making the whole look sculptural: a cross, perhaps, between an Easter Island statue and a polished Brancusi bronze.

This is not as farfetched as it sounds, though the scale of the object is at odds, of course, with those two sculptures—much smaller than the former, much larger than the latter. I cannot imagine that a musician with a cello to transport could lift and handle the whole easily; the case seems more like a coffin within which has been laid to rest the music-making artifact.

So the object I now celebrate is not the cello itself. In my father-in-law's recordings, I can hear the instrument's sound; in publicity and illustrative photographs I retain its likeness. But the actual Countess of Stanlein ex-Paganini Stradivarius violoncello of 1707 now resides in Canada, purchased by a Canadian foundation with a view to preservation, and the sponsorship of young virtuoso artists. Its afterimage becomes the image here: a wooden catafalque. What remains is the container and not the thing contained.

Writing these pages has taken some time. The stress test I predicted as four days hence in a previous passage is well behind me now. The result thereof, and of the echocardiogram, has shown my cardiologist (a doctor with the apt name of Engel—which means, in German, "angel") that I do indeed have blockages but nothing over-serious. The two technicians who supervised my procedure assured me, "You did fine." I must monitor my intake of food and increase my exercise regime, but there's no need for surgery. As my elder brother, also a doctor, observes, "If you have something wrong with you, let it be the heart. That, we do know how to fix."

So there's been a stay of execution, and brightness failed to fall. Again I feel that melding of transience and tradition which has been my subject. As with the "Litany" by Thomas Nashe, a poem stays with me, this one an epitaph from *Poems from the Greek Anthology*, translated by Dudley Fitts. It reads in its entirety:

> In my nineteenth year the darkness drew me down.
> And, ah, the sweet sun!

And here by way of coda is a companion text from Walter Savage Landor, who died at eighty-nine:

> I strove with none, for none was worth my strife:
> Nature I loved, and, next to Nature, Art;
> I warm'd both hands before the fire of Life;
> It sinks, and I am ready to depart.

To end with this couplet and then Landor's quatrain is to celebrate the legacy of those who wrote before. The author of the epitaph for that drowned nineteen-year-old remains anonymous, the old poet effectively so. We will never know the name of the first of these two writers, and Landor's name and dates (1775–1864) have small consequence today.

Still, the language lives.

ENVOI

Today is August 27—the date announced in my first sentence—and the day of my actual birthday, a way of tricking time. The composition of this book has taken one full year. I now am eighty-one.

A bird that flies from dark to dark is lit by what's between. We start and then we stop. This trope—a barn or mead hall through which the sparrow passes—is an emblem of transition. Brief transience is the theme. My art was spent describing that bright passage, and what the bird must travel through, then leave.

Tradition is our common lot; we live and then we die. We honor those who went before and dream of those to come. No one of us escapes—although there's some postponing—the necessary end.

Again, as I wrote earlier (when quoting Herodotus who was quoting Solon), "Count no man happy until the end is known." But at the provisional close of this piece—and the beginning of my ninth decade—I still proclaim myself happy. And, as always, grateful for the great good fortune of having shared this so-far journey with Elena.

ACKNOWLEDGMENTS

The author wishes to thank Robert and Dena Mandel for their scrupulous attention to and support of this book. In particular, I'm indebted to Dena Mandel for the acuity of her editorial intelligence and shaping suggestions for the text. From the first page to the final choice of title, Mandel Vilar Publishers have been everything I hoped for as collaborative sponsors, and to say that I am grateful is to understate the case. Mary Beth Hinton has revived my faith in what seemed to be the lost art of copyediting, dotting the i's and crossing the t's here throughout. Barbara Werden has been expertise itself in managing the photo inserts. And Sophie Appel splendidly designed the whole; this is a book I hope you can judge by its cover. To each and all, all thanks.

Parts of this book appeared previously in other publications: the first section of On Churchill's Chair (as "My Life in Art") in *Salmagundi* (2022–23); the most recent version of my memory of John Updike, in *Curiouser and Curiouser: Essays* (2017); the first memory of John Gardner, in my Editor's Introduction to his posthumously published *Stillness and Shadows* (1986); the passage on James Baldwin, in *Running in Place: Scenes from the South of France* (1989). These appreciations were then collected in *Why Writing Matters* (2020). Excerpts were also taken from "A Visit to the Gallery," published in *Raritan* magazine and then revised for inclusion in *Anywhere Out of the World: Essays* (2005). Reflections on the parent-child relationship appeared in the essay "A Prayer for the Daughters," included in *Fathering Daughters: Reflections by Men*, edited by DeWitt Henry and James Alan McPherson (1998); and a revised version, in *The Lost Suitcase: Reflections on the Literary Life* (2000). The memory of Max Eastman first appeared as "Reprise," in *On the Vineyard*, edited by Peter Simon (1980), and most recently revised for *Lastingness: The Art of Old Age* (2011).

ALSO BY NICHOLAS DELBANCO

FICTION

It Is Enough

The Years

Sherbrookes (single volume)

The Count of Concord

Spring and Fall

The Vagabonds

What Remains

Old Scores

In the Name of Mercy

The Writers' Trade & Other Stories

About My Table & Other Stories

Stillness

Sherbrookes

Possession

ALSO BY NICHOLAS DELBANCO

Small Rain

Fathering

In the Middle Distance

News

Consider Sappho Burning

Grasse 3/23/66

The Martlet's Tale

NONFICTION

Why Writing Matters

Curiouser and Curiouser: Essays

The Art of Youth: Crane, Carrington, Gershwin
& the Nature of First Acts

Lastingness: The Art of Old Age

Anywhere Out of the World: Essays on Travel, Writing, Death

The Countess of Stanlein Restored:
A History of the Countess of Stanlein
ex-Paganini Stradivarius Violoncello of 1707

The Lost Suitcase: Reflections on the Literary Life

Running in Place: Scenes from the South of France

The Beaux Arts Trio: A Portrait

Group Portrait: Joseph Conrad, Stephen Crane,
Ford Madox Ford, Henry James, and H. G. Wells